The Knight-Errant of Assisi

The Knight-Errant
of Assisi

BY

THE MOST REV. HILARIN FELDER, O.F.M.CAP., S.T.D.
TITULAR BISHOP OF GERA

TRANSLATED BY

THE REV. BERCHMANS BITTLE, O.F.M.CAP.

THE BRUCE PUBLISHING COMPANY
MILWAUKEE

Nihil obstat: Celestine Bittle, O.F.M.Cap.
Pacificus Raith, O.F.M.Cap.
Imprimi potest: Edmund Kramer, O.F.M.Cap., Prov.
Nihil obstat: John A. Schulien, S.T.D.
Imprimatur: ✝ Moyses E. Kiley, Archiepiscopus Milwaukiensis
4 June, 1948

Author's Foreword

THE title of this book has not been chosen by the author but by the oldest biographers of St. Francis. Thomas de Celano calls him "the new knight of Christ," "the most valiant knight of Christ" (Cel. II, 21; I, 9. 36. 72). The Three Companions likewise describe him as "the knight of Christ," who "enters the fray wearing Christ's armor" (Socii 17). St. Bonaventure also calls him "a soldier of Christ," "the new champion of Christ," "the intrepid knight of Christ," "the indefatigable knight of Christ," "the invincible leader and captain of the knights of Christ" (Bonav. I, 4. 5; II, 2; IX, 7; XIII, 9–10).

Later scholars, too, have pointed out the knightly features in the portrait of Francis, most forcibly perhaps the author of this book himself. Of late the desire for a monograph on the theme of the knighthood of the Poverello has been expressed repeatedly. Thus only recently the gifted and learned littérateur Louis Gillet wrote: *"Quel livre à faire sur François le Paladin!"* (What a book could be written on Francis the Knight!) However, up to the present time this has remained only a pious wish, although the personality and the nature of the Umbrian patriarch is revealed in full only from the viewpoint of his knighthood of Christ.

His life as a knight of Christ is divided into two periods. In the first his knighthood is formed and developed; in the second it is fully proved on the field of combat.

The development of his knighthood can be traced step by step by means of pertinent historical sources. Having been born in the age and the world of knighthood when it was in full flowering, and having been pursued by worldly dreams of becoming a prince and a paladin, Francis is drawn deeper and deeper into the ranks of the "fighting forces" of Christ, into Christ's "militia," and he is finally consecrated a knight by the "Emperor of heaven" Himself.

From this moment he proves himself a hero, a true paladin, a champion of the Lord of hosts. Instead of taking the field astride a proud charger, in shining armor and under flying banners, he puts on "the armor of God, the breastplate of justice, the shield of faith, the helmet of salvation and the sword of the spirit" (Eph. 6:13-17), and does battle until death under the banner of the cross.

This he does with knightly sentiment, in a knightly manner, and according to knightly standards; he spiritualizes the knightly ideal which he cherished in his youthful days, but in doing so he does not negate this ideal. His heart and his mind are dedicated irrevocably to the ideals of knightliness, and his life in Christ and for Christ, far from being hampered by his knighthood, is on the contrary immeasurably enhanced by it. It is the knightly element which gives to the personality of the Little Poor Man its wholly peculiar, yes, its wholly unique character.

It is the purpose of this book to demonstrate this. Its material is drawn mainly from well-known sources as well as from hitherto published Franciscan literature, including my earlier work, entitled *The Ideals of St. Francis.* From this wealth of material, however, this book selects the specifically knightly features, reduces them to a common plane, views them in their organic relationship and cohesion, and places them in the original framework from which they have grown.

Thus this book becomes a complement and an elaboration of an earlier work of mine, *The Ideals of St. Francis.* The aim and purpose of both is to bring about a better understanding and a closer imitation of the Seraphic Saint.

This book was written by the author as a votive gift for his golden sacerdotal jubilee, and it is hereby presented to the Seraphic

Father with the simple lines of Squire Lamprecht of Regensburg (1240–1255):

Sant Francisk, ich bitte dich	Saint Francis, I beg of thee
durch die grôzen heilekeit,	By that great holiness
die got an dich hât geleit,	Which God in thee has shown,
daz dû got bites umbe mich,	That thou wilt pray God for me,
daz er mîn leben kêre an sich.	That He make all my life His own.

Fribourg, Switzerland
September 21, 1940

THE AUTHOR

Translator's Note

IN PRESENTING this English version of *Der Christusritter aus Assisi* the translator feels that it will be warmly welcomed by the countless admirers and lovers of the great Umbrian saint. The author, Bishop Hilarin Felder, O.F.M.Cap., now an octogenarian, is not a stranger to the English-speaking world. He first became known many years ago as an outstanding theologian and apologete by his excellent work: *Jesus Christus* (translated by John L. Stoddard under the title: *Christ and the Critics*). But the author has also gained wide renown as a Franciscan scholar. His classic work on the Poverello: *Die Ideale des hl. Franziskus* (*The Ideals of St. Francis,* translated by Berchmans Bittle, O.F.M.Cap.) appeared almost twenty-five years ago and was heralded as a priceless contribution to the already rich treasure of Franciscan literature. It gave evidence of the scholarly attainments of the author as well as of his deep understanding and warm love of St. Francis and of all things pertaining to him and to his Order.

Simple as was the personality of the Poverello, it was nonetheless one of many facets. In the present volume the author brings new light to bear on one of these facets and makes it sparkle with brilliant radiance. Francis as the child of the age of chivalry, as the knight-errant, the paladin of Christ, stands forth in this book in much brighter colors. It is not a new Francis, but a Francis in new splendor, clothed in the shining habiliments of a knight of Christ, endowed with all the captivating qualities of a true paladin of Christ, and reflecting in his person and his actions all the glory of heroic Christian knighthood.

To show all this has been the purpose and the accomplishment of the author. To bring this also to the knowledge of the English-speaking world, as it has been brought to the knowledge of the speakers of many other tongues, has been the privilege and the endeavor of the translator. He has followed the original as closely as possible and has taken only one liberty, that of transferring the numerous notes of mere reference to the end of the book, while retaining the notes of an explanatory nature as footnotes. It is felt that by this compromise nothing of the scholarliness of the book is sacrificed, while at the same time the general reader will be able to follow a practically unbroken text and thus find his reading less hampered.

Like the author, the translator hopes and prays that his labors will help many to a better understanding of the unique personality of the great knight-errant of Assisi and induce them to emulate him in his loving, unswerving loyalty to his and their Liege Lord.

BERCHMANS BITTLE, O.F.M.CAP.

Contents

PART ONE

THE FORMING OF
THE KNIGHT-ERRANT OF CHRIST

PART TWO

THE PROVING OF
THE KNIGHT-ERRANT OF CHRIST

PART ONE

THE FORMING OF
THE KNIGHT-ERRANT OF CHRIST

CHAPTER ONE

The Age and World of Chivalry

FRANCIS and knighthood! At first blush it would seem that these two had nothing in common. Here the Poor Little Man of Assisi, so immersed in God and lost to the world, so humble and gentle, a lover of lambs and brother of all creatures; there the knight on his mettlesome charger, clothed in armor, with shield and sword and spear, the symbol of bravery and prowess in arms, of political might and bitter feuds!

This contrast is all the sharper for those — and their number is still great — who see knighthood embodied and travestied in *Don Quixote,* the immortal masterpiece of the Spanish king of poets, Miguel de Cervantes Saavedra (1547–1616). What a contrast between the saintly Patriarch and "the knight of the woeful countenance"! Don Quixote, who in his buffoonery releases robbers, fights windmills and sheep, and vanquishes the barber whose basin he regards as the helmet of Mambino; Sancho Panza, Quixote's rotund squire, who clings to a sausage in the face of his master's eccentricities, who pokes around in the fog with his lance and splinters his spear against laughable obstacles: where in this picture can be found even a trace of that much-vaunted glory of chivalry? What can this caricature have in common with the Poverello of Assisi?

Cervantes, however, was far from lampooning genuine knighthood in the person of Don Quixote; he himself had been wounded in the battle of Lepanto and had proved that he was a genuine knight as well as a true Franciscan from the crown of his head to the soles of his feet.* What he described with such angry displeasure and branded with such mordant satire was a *degenerate knighthood,* the knighthood of fantastic adventures, of enchanted castles and passionate love affairs, the knighthood as described in the inane and erotic romances of the end of the Middle Ages.

Genuine knighthood had nothing in common with such aberrations and excrescences. It had developed under the guidance of the Church. Together with the Christianizing of the German and Romanic tribes the Church transformed the wild warriors into Christian soldiers with the end in view of crushing Islam, the arch-enemy of Christendom. In order to meet the mounted Saracens on equal terms the warriors of the West had gone into battle almost exclusively on horse ever since the ninth century. They were henceforth knights, or *chevaliers,* a word derived from the French *cheval,* horse; Latin *caballus.* Even the Latin term *miles,* which up till then had designated a foot soldier, now became applicable to a mounted warrior. Yet it needed two centuries of cultural and churchly training to develop those splendid figures which fully expressed the ideal of Christian knighthood. Mere bodily strength and physical prowess, bravery and fearlessness in the face of the enemy and the mastery of arms did not yet make the knight. Indispensable was humility and loyalty; discipline and modesty; a delicate regard for the weak, the poor, the innocent; generosity and the readiness to fight for all that men held dear and sacred.[1] It was therefore said of a true knight: "No better name could be found for a perfect man than that of a knight."[2]

The special characteristics of a knight, however, were a deep sense of faith, fiery enthusiasm for Christ and a readiness to battle for His kingdom on earth. Ever since the tenth century the squire was raised to the rank of knighthood by an act of consecration on the part of the Church. The prayer which accompanied his girding with the sword was as follows: "Hear, O Lord, our prayers and with the hand of Thy Majesty bless this sword with which Thy servant desires to be girded, so that he may defend and guard the

---

* Cervantes was a member of the Third Order of St. Francis. As a Tertiary he wrote the second part of his *Don Quixote* in 1615. The first part had appeared in 1605. — Numbered notes will be found in reference section at end of book.

churches, the widows, the orphans and all the servants of God against the cruelty of the barbarians and may become a terror for all who lie in wait for him." The Bishop then blessed the sword and handed it to the new knight with the words: "Receive this sword in the name of the Father, and of the Son, and of the Holy Ghost, and employ it to defend yourself and the holy Church of God, as well as to fight the enemies of the cross and of the Christian faith."[3] The first two commandments of the decalogue of the knight were: "You shall believe all things the Church teaches, and observe all things she commands you. You shall defend the Church."[4] Every morning, when the knight assisted at Mass, he drew his sword from its scabbard when the Gospel was read and held it upright in his hands until the reading was over. This proud posture was to express the firm sentiment: "Whenever the defense of the Gospel or of the Church is at stake, I am ready." To pledge the last drop of his blood for the preservation and the spread of God's kingdom: that was the first purpose and the final aim of knighthood. Knighthood was the armed force in the service of unarmed truth.* It reached its greatest heights in the Crusades (1095–1270), that gigantic struggle against Islam advancing in the West, the South, and the East. The massed armies of Islam threatened to engulf the entire Occident, to destroy Church and empire, to submerge culture and civilization. All Christendom felt itself deeply wounded by the occupation and shameful desecration of the holy places in Palestine on the part of its archenemy. Conditions in the Holy Land under the rule of the Seljuk Turks (since 1073) became intolerable as well for the Christian inhabitants as for visiting pilgrims. The might of the Crescent had to be broken at any cost, the holy places cried out to be redeemed. Clergy and laity rose up in fiery indignation, determined to solve this formidable problem once for all.

---

* "Knighthood in the eyes of the Church has never been, is not now, and never will be other than an armed force in the service of unarmed truth. And I am not aware that a loftier or more exact definition has ever been given. (La Chevalerie, aux yeux de l'Eglise, n'a jamais été, elle n'est encore, elle ne sera jamais que la force armée au service de la vérité désarmée. Et je ne sache pas qu'on en ait jamais donné une plus haute, une plus exacte définition.)" Gautier, loc. cit., p. 48.

Leading all the rest, the knights took up the cross, resolved to conquer or to die for Christ. No doubt some of them were led by an urge for action and a romantic love of adventure. But the soul of the earlier Crusades was after all pure, religious enthusiasm, such as had never been witnessed before. It was this alone which induced the crusaders to leave wife and children, home and court and country, and to take upon themselves untold toil and hardship. Nothing else was of any account whenever there was a question of proving themselves as "God's vassals," as "heroes of the Lord God." In the midst of unspeakable sufferings and deprivations the cry rose from their ranks: "May we be deemed worthy to see Jerusalem, to sing the *Kyrie* and *Gloria* before its holy walls and to kiss the ground with the joyous cry: Jesus has passed here!"[5] "Even if the walls of Jerusalem were forged of steel, we would bite them open with our teeth!" was the cry from the ranks of Godfrey of Bouillon.[6] "Even if we were already in paradise, we would come down to fight against the Saracens," exclaimed the brave warriors.[7] They died with the sigh on their lips: "Jesus of Nazareth, sweet Lord Jesus Christ!"[8] The Crusades did not achieve their ultimate goal; but the incalculable sacrifices which they entailed would not have been in vain if they had had but one result: to bring Christian knighthood in all its splendor and spiritual force to its fullest flowering.

With the Christian lay knighthood were closely associated also the military Orders of knights.[9] After the Holy Land had been redeemed by conquest (1099), the armies of the Crusades streamed back to the West, with the exception of a few remnants. The problem now arose of providing a strong bulwark for the newly established kingdom of Jerusalem and armed protection for the Christians living among the Moslems or visiting the places of pilgrimage. At this point the Church called into being those religious military Orders, the like of which the world had never seen. They were praying knights and armed monks, who added to the three customary vows the sacred oath to guard the roads and streets against marauders, to guide the pilgrims to the holy places and to protect them from raiders, to nurse the sick, and to give their lives bravely in defense of the Holy Land.*

St. Bernard, the author of the first Rule of the Knights Templar, describes the greatness of this religious knighthood: "Truly a new and unheard of kind of knighthood!" he exclaims. "To resist the enemy bravely in bodily conflict, that I deem not very remarkable, nor very extraordinary. That one should, on the other hand, wage war against vices and the devil with spiritual prowess is, though praiseworthy, yet not so amazing, for there are monks throughout the world who have made this their calling. But if a man girds himself with a sword to wage a twofold war, who would not deem this not only as unheard of, but also as worthy of all praise and admiration? Truly, he is the knight without fear and without reproach who clothes his body in steel and his soul in the armor of faith, who, having put on a twofold armor, fears neither devil nor man; who in life belongs to Christ, and for whom to die is gain; who throws himself at the enemy of the cross with the cry: 'In life and in death I am the Lord's!' How glorious these conquerors return from battle, how happy they succumb as martyrs! Rejoice, brave warrior, if you conquer and live in the Lord; rejoice even more if you fall in battle and enter the Kingdom of the Lord! Blessed indeed is your life and glorious your victory: but preferable to both is your holy death!"[10]

Apart from checking Islam and being active in the exercise of charity, the military Orders rendered an inestimable service by educating the nobility of the West. Above all they remained the bearers and exemplars of the Christian ideal of knighthood at a time when this began to wane.

For one cannot fail to recognize that even before the end of the twelfth century there were signs which unmistakably portended

---

* The oldest military Orders are the Knights of St. John (1113), and the Knights Templar (1119). In the second half of this century the Spanish religious Orders of knights arose, that of St. Julian (1156), the Military Order of Calatrava (1160), the Knights of St. James (1170), and the Order of Aviz (1181). Their purpose was to battle Islam in the West, as did the Knights of St. John and the Templars in the East. To the Teutonic Order, founded at Jerusalem (1190), was given the task of gaining pagan Prussia for Christianity.

the *decline of genuine knighthood*. The Crusades which had sprung from the purest religious enthusiasm, had also made the participants acquainted with the riches as well as the lax morals of the Orient and had excited in them the craving for pleasures and adventures. The returned warriors had to fill in the long pauses between the various expeditions to the East in some way. They journeyed whenever possible to various theaters of war where money, lands, and honors beckoned. If larger fields of combat were not to be found, they engaged in petty feuds or promoted warlike displays and brilliant tournaments, with which endless feasting and noisy revels went hand in hand. The private lives of the feudal classes as well as their family life left much to be desired in many instances. Many knights, it is true, remained faithful to their high calling when abroad as well as when in their castles; others, however, lapsed into an attitude and manner of life which was in direct contradiction to the ideals of a consecrated sword and the lofty standards of the Crusades.

Evidence of the luster of the original ideal of knighthood in the age of the Crusades and of its gradual dimming is found in the Frankish, Breton, and Provençal epic poetry of that era. This must be touched upon for the reason that Francis unmistakably stood under its magic influence, and also for the reason that these poems most perfectly mirrored his time and world. It is not to be wondered at that the first of these epics grew without exception from the soil of France and are composed partly in the North-Frankish language (*Langue d'oïl*), and partly in the South-French (*Langue d'oc*). France was the native land of the Crusades; France wielded spiritual leadership over the West since the eleventh century; from France sprang every creative impetus which in turn enriched the neighboring countries; in France Gothic architecture, knighthood, and chivalric poetry had its home.

Chief among the French epic poems (*chansons de geste*) was the *Song of Roland*.[11] It was written around the turn of the eleventh century in northern France, and soon after (1127–1139) a German version was made by Konrad, a Bavarian priest.[12] This grand epos tells of the legendary expedition of Charlemagne against the

Saracens in Spain and extols the victory won by him and his knights for Church and empire. King Charles is represented as the exemplar of a true hero, strong and fervent in faith. He is manly and yet gentle, a just judge, devout, humble, filled with trust in God and reverence toward God. He is the mighty rock against which the Moorish flood broke in its onslaught.

He has gathered around himself, besides his two close associates, or paladins, the wisest among his counsellors and the bravest of his knights. They are adorned with all the virtues of Christian knighthood, expert warriors, chaste and pure, brave and true, joyously ready to die for Christ and to gain heaven as martyrs. The most renowned among them are his nephew Roland, the latter's intimate friend Oliver, and Archbishop Turpin — all three ideal types of chivalric heroism: zest for battle, invincible bravery, and spiritual knighthood. In contrast to them stands the traitor, Ganelon, whose punishment is disgrace, condemnation by the people's court or *Fehme,* and eternal damnation. In the *Song of Roland* the paladins of Charlemagne appear indeed as reckless giants, proud of their physical prowess, but at the same time they are notable for their tender love of the Redeemer, their unreserved fealty to their royal Liege Lord, their hearty friendship, their ruggedly virile discipline and moral purity, their deep piety, their joyous and selfless devotedness to the King of heaven and their death-defying zeal for their holy faith.

After the middle of the twelfth century the *Song of Roland* had to give place to the Breton romantic epics. The legend of King Arthur stems from the heroic battles which the English Celts fought against the invading Anglo-Saxons in the fifth and sixth centuries.[13] From this historical kernel there sprung in the course of time prolific accretions, fabled narratives, the central point of which was the legendary King Arthur and his twelve Knights of the Round Table. The poets of northern France, from 1135 on, made them representative of the chivalric culture of their time. King Arthur is pictured as the prototype of a knightly ruler. Rich and generous, he rules over a brilliant court, reveling in the glittering splendor of his past exploits, and enjoying the exalted

position of a king with his wife Guinevere at his side. His twelve
heroes roam abroad to perform many deeds of valor. They defend
the oppressed, conquer giants, dwarfs, dragons, fairies, monsters,
and destroy all kinds of mysterious and fantastic sorcery. They
perform these deeds in the hope of being rewarded on their return
to Arthur's court with kingdoms, fame, and the favor of fair
ladies.

   Thus the heroes of King Arthur's Round Table are characterized
by lust for adventure, thirst for honors, and the amorous cult of
woman. The chivalric hero of the Arthurian romances is perhaps
one more cultured and refined than the heroes of the *Song of
Roland,* but he no longer possesses that primitive, virile, and
deeply religious spirit which animated the Germanic-Carolingian
paladins. While the Arthurian romances were driving the *Song of
Roland* more and more into the background, first in France and
soon also in Italy, Spain, Portugal, England, and Germany, the
supranational ideal of chivalry itself deteriorated and began to
sink from its lofty heights. This grievous loss, however, was com-
pensated in a measure by the fact that both Chrestien de Troyes
in his *Perceval le Gaulois* (around 1188) and Wolfram von Eschenbach (born 1170) in his German *Parzival* added to the Arthurian
romances the legend of the Holy Grail.*

---

* According to medieval legend the Holy Grail was the vessel, or chalice, used
by the Saviour at the Last Supper and in which Joseph of Arimathea gathered
drops of blood of the Crucified. He is supposed to have carried this sacred vessel
later on to Britain, where it was entrusted to the Knights of the Round Table for
safekeeping. They were therefore called the Knights of the Holy Grail. Chrestien
de Troyes, who elaborated the Arthurian legends in a number of his works, allows
their pagan character to appear in some measure even in his *Perceval le Gaulois;*
Wolfram von Eschenbach, however, "in his *Parzival* has described the real essence
and nature of the Grail, and has thus placed the highly colored adventures of the
Arthurian legends in the service of an idea of great depth, has ennobled and
consecrated the heroic deeds by their divine purpose, has sanctified earthly love
by divine love, and at the same time has solved the greatest problems of the human
mind and stilled the deepest yearnings of the human breast." P. Anselm Salzer:
Illustr. Geschichte der deutschen Litteratur, I, p. 156 (Regensburg, 1926). Regarding the Holy Grail see also the *Catholic Encyclopedia,* vol. VI. The more modern
versions of the Grail legend are Tennyson's "Holy Grail" in the *Idylls of the King*
(1869), and Wagner's music-drama *Parsifal,* produced for the first time at
Bayreuth in 1882.

Contemporary with the romantic epics of northern France the lyric poetry of the Provençal troubadours began to gain ground in southern France.[14] Its relation to medieval knighthood is evident from the fact that it rose and died with the Crusades. The earliest troubadour was William IX, Count of Poitiers and Duke of Aquitaine, who led an army to Palestine in 1101; the last of the troubadours is Guiraut Riquier, Delphin of Auvergne, whose poetic muse was stilled by death in 1294. During this span of years hundreds of troubadours arose and thousands of poems came to life, many of which have been preserved together with their musical settings. Most of the troubadours belonged to the lower (ministerial) grades of knighthood and were active in the service of the larger and smaller feudal courts. Often they were poets, composers, singers, and recitators in one. At times, however, they engaged itinerant *jongleurs* to sing their songs; in many instances the latter often sought to entertain their audiences with crude poetry and cruder comedy.

While the long and heavy epic romances of northern France excelled by reason of their idealistic content, the shorter, light-winged songs of the southern troubadours stood out by reason of the perfection of their artistic form. They were thus assured of achieving their desired purpose, which was to entertain court society. The material for these songs was furnished by various events, trivial as well as important, occurring at the court itself, the actual or legendary history of the dynasties, the political and military events of the time, or any other occurrences with which the poet had become acquainted. The troubadours were also called upon to sing the praises of knightly honor and duty: unqualified fealty, inviolable loyalty to God, to king and liege lord, heroic bravery in fighting the enemies of the faith, of home and country, of right and law, of the weak, the wronged and the oppressed. In particular, they were called upon to sing the praises of the liege lady, the mistress of the court.

The wife of the feudal lord was the pivotal point of court society. House and hearth, sanctified by sacramental marriage, the well-being of the family, the morals and welfare of the servants, food

and clothing, the furnishings of the home, the education of the
children, manners and culture, the care of the sick and of the
poor, matters of refinement and artistic adornment of the home —
all this was entrusted to the quiet and efficient administration of
the lady of the castle. For this reason everyone, from the lord to
the lowest menial, had to serve her. The court singer in particular was engaged permanently or temporarily for the service
of the liege lady. He called her outright his "lord" (*Midunz,
Dominus meus*). He had to sing the praises of her beauty, her
charm, her goodness of heart, all the magic of her physical and
spiritual excellence. He had to render homage to her in song,
sound her praises, pay court to her, make her the adored object
of his conventional love.

For this reason the troubadours were called *minnesingers,* singers
of love. The courts at which these minnesingers flourished were
called courts of love, and the entire life and doings of the troubadours and of their satellites, the *jongleurs,* went by the name of the
"gay" or "joyous science" (*gaya sciencia*).

The service and the songs of the troubadours are to be judged
according to medieval standards. The court poet directed his song
to the assembled courtiers. He was called upon by them to sing for
the amusement of the lady of the court, to entertain the courtiers
themselves, and to elevate social life to a higher, more refined
sphere. Thus the lyric poetry of the troubadours had a social character; it was a diversion full of spirit and deep sentiment, and not a
personal amorous experience or confession of love on the part of
the poet. As long as and in as far as it kept within the bounds set
by Christian morals and chivalric standards, this sort of poetry could
not be objected to seriously. The poetry of the minnesong did actually remain on this high level to a great extent. A considerable
number of troubadours took part in the Crusades and risked their
lives to deliver the grave of the Saviour from the hands of the
infidels. At times the worldly minnesong became a Crusader song.
From the love of woman the singers occasionally rose to the love of
God; yes, at times they asserted that Christian chivalry places the
love of God above the love of woman, while the pagan knighthood

of the Saracens sought its greatest fame solely in the cult of the feminine.[15]

Unfortunately, however, the minnesong of the Christian knights and troubadours only too often also sank from its high level to mere amorousness, to sultry sensuality, and even to flaming passion. This was especially the case when the general decadence of morals set in during the thirteenth century.*

In the meantime the "gay science" had long ago spread to all countries. Wherever knighthood flourished, the new movement was received with homage. Spreading out from Provence, it triumphantly conquered all of France, Castile, Aragon, Catalonia, Navarre, Portugal, Germany, and England, as well as the Latin kingdom of the Orient. It was in Italy especially that the lyric poetry of the troubadours found universal acclaim and a loud response. This is understandable since this country bordered directly on the Provence, and because the Provençal language was closely related to the Italian dialects, of which, according to Dante, there were more than a thousand in his day. The most famous troubadours of the Provence, such as Peire Vidal, Raimbaut de Vaqueiras, Americ de Peghulan, Gaucelm Faydit, Folquet de Romans, Berhard de Ventadour, spent a great part of their lives wandering about Italy and singing their songs. But Italian poets, too, employed the Provençal idiom, because they did not yet possess a native literary tongue.[16] At the court of the Hohenstaufen emperors, who often traveled from one end of Italy to the other, the troubadours found a warm welcome and generous patrons. The feudal lords of Este, Verona, Montferrat, and Ferrara, too, soon had their own "courts of love."

When finally, toward the end of the twelfth century, one city after another began to throw off the yoke of the feudal lords, courtly customs and manners became prevalent together with the newly won civil liberties. Treviso, Venice, Genoa, Florence, Ancona vied

---

* Most of the troubadours, who still flourished until the end of the thirteenth century, "fostered the genuine minnesong in its ancient form, glorifying duchesses and court ladies, complaining sadly of their coldness and infidelity, primness and disdain, sighing for warm glances and reciprocated love, discoursing with other poets on the rules and the vicissitudes of love." Baumgartner, loc. cit., VI, p. 30.

with one another in staging glittering pageants and popular entertainments. Grand tournaments and spirited jousts were conducted in the public places. These were given a lighter touch and a certain refinement by the songs and music of the troubadours and jongleurs. As soon as the sound of the voice and the lute was stilled, however, combats and jousts once more took possession of the arena. In the larger cities such festivities followed one another almost without interruption and not even the frequent feuds and wars were able to bring them to a halt. In smaller towns the "golden youth" came together for merrymaking, in emulation of the noisy festivities of the larger cities. On every road one could meet itinerant singers and musicians with a lyre or a lute on their backs. Castles opened their gates to them. Courtiers and servants listened avidly to their songs. Their almost endless verses and refrains were received everywhere with generous acclaim.

The lyric poetry of the Provence was joined by the classical hero epics of northern France. Pilgrims who traveled in an unbroken procession to Rome on the "French roads" (*Viae Francigenae, vie francesche*), and who were accompanied by singers and musicians from France (*cantatores Francigenorum*), very early brought the *chansons de geste* to the South.[17] That the *Song of Roland* appeared in Italy after the twelfth century can be established from many sources.[18] The treachery of Ganelon against Roland and Oliver and the defeat at Roncesvalle are mentioned already in 1131 in a public inscription to be seen at Nepi, and therefore very close to Umbrian territory.[19] Not a few traces of the Arthurian legend can also be found. Frequently the names of the Knights of the Round Table were given in baptism in place of the names of the saints.[20] On the vault of the cathedral of Modena (twelfth century) several knights together with King Arthur are carved in high relief, picturing them in an assault on a castle.[21]

The paladins of the Breton and Carolingian romances were extremely popular figures. The heroic exploits ascribed to them were regarded as indubitably historic and were spread among high and low in narrative and song.[22] It will be seen that Francis, too, was well acquainted with the *Song of Roland*, the legend of King Arthur and with the "gay science" of the troubadours, and that he was carried away by the magic charm of chivalric poetry.

In fact, Francis of Assisi was born directly into this age and world of minstrelsy with its song and music. Knighthood in all its forms and with all its heroic figures wooed his romantic soul. That he did not become a victim of that knighthood which had already fallen from its high estate, that he not only made real the Christian ideal of knightliness, but became a knight-errant of Christ in the full sense of the word, that is the secret of his life.

CHAPTER TWO

Between the Yardstick and the Sword

FRANCIS of Assisi first saw the light of this world in the spring of the year 1182. Lucius III was the reigning pontiff and Frederick Barbarossa ruled the empire. The glamour of knighthood and of chivalric poetry shed its magic light over his cradle.*

But he himself was not born to knighthood. Only those were held to be born to shield and sword whose parents and grandparents had been members of the knightly estate. This was not true of Francis. The circumstances of his station and parentage, however, made him eligible to knighthood.

In exceptional cases knights were recruited from all stations of life. Every brave man of good character could under certain circumstances achieve the goal of knighthood. Usually, however, the knights came from the ranks of the nobles or of wealthy merchants. Whoever was of noble blood was by that very fact a candidate for knighthood, in as far as he was fitted by reason of a good reputation and military prowess. Thus it happened that the feudal nobility and the knightly estate became of almost equal rank. Many knights, however, had risen from the merchant class, on condition, however, that they were able to live in the manner of gentlemen and were not dependent for their livelihood on manual labor. Furthermore, the equipment of a knight and the upkeep of men and horses in the

---

* Fr. Dominic Mandic, O.F.M. (*De Protoregula Fratrum Minorum,* Mostar, 1923, pp. 4-19) has established beyond a doubt that the conversion of Francis took place between January 1 and March 19, 1207. Thomas of Celano, however, asserts that Francis at that time was about 25 years old. Most likely, therefore, he was born in the early part of the year 1182.

field was so costly that it could be furnished only by the wealthy. Many tradespeople, however, especially the wholesale merchants, were very rich. They were often bankers and money lenders, upon whom the nobility itself was often dependent. In some sections, as for instance in the Provence, the merchants were considered as nobility of the second class, and for this reason the ranks of knighthood were open to them. Only one thing was demanded of them: the merchant had to sell the cloth in wholesale lots and metal by the hundredweight and not by ounces and pounds, as the small tradespeople.[1] In central Italy particularly, as in Florence, Perugia, Assisi, the government of the civic republics passed largely into the hands of the merchant guilds, and thus the distinction between the feudal nobility and the merchant class almost disappeared.[*]

In view of this Francis had an established right to prospective knighthood. His mother Pica was a noblewoman. In the documents of the notariate she is always mentioned as Donna, Domina, Madonna, or "Lady," an incontrovertible proof that she was of noble descent.[2] In her person great nobility of heart and mind was joined to nobility of birth. Gentle, meek, benevolent, charitable, devout of heart, and cheerful of spirit, she stood out as a model of all womanly virtue.[3] Her husband, Peter Bernardone, was a wholesale cloth merchant, who by means of his trade had succeeded in reaching the heights as one of the richest and most influential citizens of Assisi.[4] His warehouse occupied a place in the main square of the city, and his business faced a future all the brighter since the cloth trade had risen to a privileged place in the communal enterprises of Assisi.[5] It followed naturally that his social life became interwoven with that of all classes of society, including barons and knights.

His trade beyond the confines of Assisi did the rest. The merchants of those days were on the road for the greater part of the year, visiting famous markets. In some places these markets were in operation almost continuously and lured buyers and sellers from

---

[*] Cf. Arnold Fortini, *Nova vita di San Francesco d'Assisi* (Milano, 1926), 56; Fortini, the *sindaco* of Assisi and enthusiastic admirer of St. Francis, has the merit of having exploited the archives of the city to the full in the endeavor to gather all local material for the life of the saint.

the most remote parts of Europe. On their journeys the merchants generally sought out the manors and the castles of the knights and took shelter there, since there were few inns and the roads were none too safe. Their appearance was always an event for the lords and their ladies. They brought news from strange places and foreign countries and offered the welcome opportunity of making the necessary purchases to replenish dwindling stocks.

This was especially true of cloth merchants. Through the Crusades the West had come to know and love the fine Oriental fabrics and tapestries. Already shortly after the capture of Jerusalem (1099) the Crusaders found that they could not do without them, so that St. Bernard complained that the knights were caparisoned and decked out with womanish vanity. Men and horses shone with the luster of precious silk fabrics; the latter were adorned with gold and precious stones and often flowed to the ground so that, during a gallop, mount and rider were enveloped in a cloud of dust. This luxury of dress had reached such a height that the warriors wore these gorgeous garments even over their armor when about to go into battle to fight and to die.[6]

In the manors and castles, too, this oriental pomp and splendor was to be found. Halls and rooms were covered with exquisite fabrics. One actually walked on silks and satins, woven for the greater part in Brabant, Flanders, and Holland, and promenaded between walls hung with gay-colored tapestries, which had been imported from Greece, Syria, Persia, and Sicily. The greatest displays were occasioned by the frequent tournaments for which hundreds, yes, thousands of knights assembled. As these vied to outshine each other by physical prowess and zest for combat, so no less by the finery and wealth of their attire. Luxury and love of finery soon infected also the citizens of the towns. It is easy to understand therefore that the cloth merchants were not only the wealthiest, but also the most respected of their class. Their heavily laden wagons rolled on all the roads from southern Italy to the famous cloth markets of northern France, and especially of Champagne, where the exchange of goods between northern and southern Europe took place.[7]

While Peter Bernardone was on such a journey, his wife, Pica, bore him a son. The happy mother had the child brought to the Cathedral of San Rufino to be baptized, giving him the name of John Baptist.[8] But when the father, on his return from France, beheld his newborn son, he called him Francesco, which meant as much as "French" in the prevalent Italian idiom. There was indeed no saint of that name; however, at that time not much attention was given to the Church calendar, and the name Francesco furthermore occurred quite frequently in and around Assisi.[9] Bernardone no doubt chose this name in memory of "gentle France," the land of profitable business and of enchanting knighthood. Perhaps he also had the future career of his first-born son in mind, for he had ambitious plans for him. As the father himself, so was his little "Frenchman" to become a merchant eligible to the knighthood, closely related to the nobility and yet without exchanging the lucrative business of cloth merchant for the glamorous but costly profession of arms. He did not dream that the proverbial saying: "From the yardstick to the sword," was already playing an important role in the boy's life.

The first training of the child was in the hands of the mother. Bernardone was often absent on business and even at home he was completely absorbed in it. Pica planted in the heart of her beloved son the fear of God and a love of purity, generosity, and true nobility of soul, all excellent qualities which she herself possessed in a high degree and which Francis was to retain in spite of his later extravagant manner of living. But with the excellent qualities of her noble descent Pica also transmitted to her child certain weaknesses found in higher society. The Crusades had furthered the appetite of the upper classes for luxury and pleasures. Furthermore, in the twelfth and thirteenth centuries the cities of Italy had progressed very rapidly. They had become free and strong. Side by side with the dismal poverty which held the lower classes in its grip, love of finery, craving for amusements and pleasures, worldly ways and a worldly spirit in all forms had taken hold among the higher classes. In the wealthy families of nobles and citizens even children became infected with these vicious tendencies, or were purposely urged to follow this manner of life. No doubt, Donna Pica believed it due to her noble lineage to educate her son according to the views and principles of her station. Her husband was all the more in agreement with this since he regarded himself as closely related to the nobility, due to his marriage and to his position as a wealthy merchant. Thus Francis grew up as a much-pampered and luxury-loving young gentleman.*

The boy Francis received his elementary education at the hands of the priests of St. George.[10] St. George's was not far from the Bernardone residence and was at the same time church, hospital, school, and chamber of commerce, and its nearness made it very suitable for the education of the young scholar.[11] The course of studies as well as the objective of such schools was very modest. Their main purpose was to teach the pupils piety, discipline, good manners, and proper deportment. They also learned to read and write. The so-called *tabula* was used for this purpose, that is, a primer with the alphabet and some reading matter, the Creed, the Our Father, and other prayers. The main object was to enable the pupils to read the Psalter, which was the common prayer book, and to memorize it.[12] At the same time some knowledge of the Latin tongue was imparted, since at that time this language was used in preaching, in the courts, and in business. It was understood by almost everyone, since it was closely related to the Old Italian dialect.[13] The elementary school finally imparted some knowledge of French, which was the language of chivalric literature and of the French court.

This was actually the education which Francis received. He could read and write.[14] Not very proficiently, however, and for this reason he usually dictated his writings in later years and signed them with a simple T, the symbol of the cross of Christ.[15] There is only one autograph of his extant, and that is the blessing which he wrote down for his confessor and secretary, Brother Leo; the writing betrays a very unpracticed hand. Francis also knew Latin, so that he

---

* Cel., I, 1–2. Here Thomas of Celano paints in colors that are too glaring, according to the custom of hagiographers of the time, in order to bring the conversion of Francis into stronger light later on. In the *Vita* II, 3, he himself corrects this exaggeration.

was able not only to follow the liturgical texts fairly well,[16] but also to dictate letters[17] and other writings in this language.[18] He spoke and sang preferably in French, though not with any degree of fluency.[19] He was not a learned man, and much less a man of science. Nature had, indeed, endowed him with a lively imagination, a faithful memory, and a clear and rapid perception. He was equipped with such a rich fund of talents that he could have risen to the heights in any field of human endeavor, be that in learning, art, or any other sphere of achievement.[20] But this did not concern him. He was destined to become a merchant and a knight. What he had learned at St. George's, was exactly the educational level of the merchant class and of the nobility.* There is no doubt that he felt himself attracted even then by these young noblemen and their courtly manners.

At an early age, however, he was admitted into his father's business and gave promise of becoming an excellent merchant.** He had a quick grasp for business details, charming affability, adaptability, and natural shrewdness.[21] These qualities would have enabled him to augment the family fortunes in a measurable degree, but he had remarkably little interest for this. He had the unbusinesslike fault of spending money like water. "He was," remarks Thomas of Celano, "not avaricious, but spendthrifty, not an amasser of wealth but a waster of riches, a shrewd merchant indeed, but at the same time a liberal giver."[22]

This was an outgrowth of his schooling for the knighthood. The knight had to excel in *courtoisie* or "courtliness." This term had a much wider scope in those days than now. While at present it denotes primarily conventional forms of deportment and is used in the sense of courtesy, it designated in the Middle Ages the entire concept of high-minded principle and manner of conduct as it was in vogue at the feudal courts and prescribed by the chivalric code of honor. The main characteristic of *courtoisie* was, however, kind-

---

* The assumption that knights and feudal lords were illiterate can no longer be upheld, as Gautier, *loc. cit.,* p. 143 ff., definitely proves.

** The Italian text of the Three Companions, ed. Amoni, p. 11, states that he was then fourteen years of age. (*Questo, poichè fu adulto, cioè di anni quattordici. . . .*)

heartedness, generosity, munificence. The knight was constantly admonished to avoid every appearance of avarice and niggardliness, to spend with both hands, never to count, always to give whenever an occasion was offered.[28] All service rendered to the poor and oppressed was looked upon by the medieval knight as service rendered to Christ Himself.

From his earliest youth, Francis was deeply imbued with the ideal of knightly deportment. *"Courtoisie,"* the Three Companions write, "was inborn in him, as it were," and his motto therefore was: "If you are generous and courtly towards men from whom you can expect nothing but a vain and passing favor, then it is only just that for love of God, who rewards with boundless generosity, you be courtly and generous also towards the poor."[24]

Only once, when he was completely absorbed in a business deal, did he forget himself and repulse a poor man who had asked an alms *"per amor di Dio"* — for the love of God. But he had hardly become aware of his action when he accused himself of a gross misdemeanor, and, touched by God's grace, he exclaimed: "If that poor man had asked for something in behalf of a count or baron, you surely would have given it to him; how much more ought you to have done it for the King of kings and the Lord of all!"[25] The deeply religious sensibility of Francis saw in the poor beggar even in those early days an ambassador of the Most High, and with a truly chivalric sense he felt it to be a very discourteous act not to have rated this ambassador above the local nobility and not to have received him with royal honors. This thought filled him with such a sense of remorse that he ran after him and after overtaking him he gave him a generous alms; furthermore he vowed never in future to refuse a request made for the love of God, a vow which he kept inviolate to the day of his death.[26]

Besides the knightly qualities of benevolence and generosity, Francis also had a great love for the "gay science" of the troubadors. How often had not Bernardone spoken of the gay doings of the minstrels and troubadours! How vividly he described the tournaments and other festive pageants of the knights when he returned from a journey to France! Was it any wonder that Francis whether awake or asleep dreamed only of this romantic life? In fact he was witness of this merry life in Assisi itself. In his days the troubadours traversed Italy from north to south, tournaments and gay entertainments for the masses were almost daily occurrences, "courts of love" arose in all larger cities, and in the smaller ones "golden youth" banded together to foster the *gaya sciencia*. A master, or *Podestà*, chosen by the group, lured the joyous band from feast to feast, from revel to revel, often to frivolity and licentiousness. The communal statutes of Assisi gave him the right to assess the cost of a feasting against any member of the band, with the provision that a payment of not more than ten *soldi* could be levied on an individual.[27] In order to escape payment the members of such a band would usually elect a wealthy and openhanded master or leader, one who was willing and able to defray the cost of their feastings.

The leader of Assisian youth toward the end of the twelfth century was none other than the son of Peter Bernardone. Wealthy, generous, and full of the joy of life, he had all the qualities necessary to play his role with success. In fact, he took such great delight in playing this role that he had little time or inclination for serious matters. If he happened to be standing behind the counter and saw his boon companions on the street, he was unable to hold back. With a scepter in his hand he marched at their head through the streets, singing the songs of the French troubadours and engaging in all sorts of merrymaking. They would often enter an inn and amuse themselves with drinking and banqueting, filling the air with songs and gay music. And long after the more sedate citizens had gone to sleep, the merry revelers once more began their noisy rounds.[28]

Francis was always the gayest of the gay. The most daring ideas always came from him. But he alone also paid the bills. "He was," remarks Thomas of Celano, "the first in banter, in jests, in merry nonsense and jovial talk, in droll songs, and also in soft and flowing garments."[29] The Three Companions add that in his exuberance he had a costume made for himself from precious goods and coarse material, solely for the purpose of attracting attention and of appearing like a troubadour.[30]

But despite his jovial and merry disposition, his vanity and love of amusement, he avoided all that was base and vulgar. He was never guilty of a loose word, much less of indelicate actions. His companions knew this and acted accordingly. But if someone happened to make an offensive remark, Francis broke off all speech and punished the offender with an icy silence.[31] To this sense of purity and moral delicacy was joined the courtly spirit of a young gentleman. He possessed rare gentleness and meekness, unusual patience and obligingness, and in general his deportment was altogether charming and captivating. He had made a special resolve never to pass harsh judgments on others and never to speak disparagingly of others.[32]

In a general way all this was evidence that the merchant's son was developing into a true knight. At first his parents were overjoyed at seeing the grand manner in which Francis cultivated the "gay science." They were pleased to see him march at the head of Assisi's "golden youth" and to notice his being looked upon with wonder by the townspeople. They did not, of course, hide from him their misgivings over his spendthrift ways but they put no obstacles in his way, realizing that he was, as the Three Companions relate, "as if by nature courtly in his speech and manner."[33] Donna Pica especially with a mother's premonition felt great confidence in the high-mindedness and moral purity of her favorite son and promised him a great future.[34] Bernardone, too, felt flattered by the popularity of Francis. Having an eye for the interests of his business, he insisted that his prospective successor and heir cultivate a close acquaintanceship with the higher classes.

But his attitude changed when Francis began to squander his profits, neglect his work, and become more and more a stranger to the shop. Now Bernardone's hopes of making his first-born an able successor in business faded rapidly. With a great deal of justice on his side he reproached Francis: "You make a display as if you were not the son of a cloth merchant, but a born prince."[35] However, no matter how often these reproaches were repeated, they merely confirmed the son and heir in his ways. Soon there developed between father and son that crossing of purposes which had always separated the sword from the yardstick.

Just because it had become so easy to rise from the merchant class to the rank of knighthood, many tradespeople of the middle classes were forced into a bitter conflict with their sons who aspired to a higher level of society. Such family feuds were so frequent that they became typical of the plots found in the chivalric romances. Thus, for example, in the *geste* of Herviz of Metz, the Roland of Lorraine. Herviz, son of the noblewoman Aelis and of the citizen Thierry, was destined to become a merchant like his father. But all the efforts of Thierry were in vain. Instead of trading in furs, in cloths from Flanders and jewels from Paris in the market at Provins, Herviz dissipated the greater part of the money received from his father in feasting and banqueting; with the rest he bought a horse, falcons, and dogs, and spent his time at hunting and taking part in tournaments. Neither pleadings nor punishments could bring him to his senses; he became a hero as a knight-errant and finally died as a Crusader at the grave of the Saviour.[36]

There is great probability that Francis had heard of this and similar *chansons de geste* and that he sang them, just as he actually did sing the *Song of Roland* and the songs of King Arthur and his Round Table.[37] These romantic songs of heroic knight-errants struck a vibrant chord in his own heart; their echo resounded throughout the golden days of his youth when he walked the streets of Assisi as a merry troubadour.[38] The pattern of chivalry and of knight-errantry had enmeshed itself in his soul.

CHAPTER THREE

The Knight-Novice Is Tested

FRANCIS was soon to become acquainted with the serious side of knighthood and soldiering. His youthful years occurred in that turbulent period in which the cities of Italy threw off the yoke of feudal domination. Assisi won its struggle for freedom at the turn of the twelfth century. This event took place under circumstances which were to be decisive for the future fortunes of Francis.[1]

His native city on the western slope of Monte Subasio dominated the Umbrian countryside from Perugia in the north to Spoleto in the south. For this reason alone it was an apple of contention between alien tyrants, the neighboring cities and native despots. When the German emperors in the eleventh and twelfth centuries forced almost the entire Italian peninsula and Sicily under their yoke, Assisi was also occupied by them. The city, indeed, received the promise that it would be freed of the oppression by local despots and would be subject only to the emperor and his officials. But instead of that it was forced to bear the harshness of the imperial rule, as well as the tyranny of the petty feudal nobles allied with it. Resentment over this treatment grew hotter from day to day and finally boiled over into a rebellion against the sovereignty of the emperor. Frederick Barbarossa (1152–1190) laid siege to the recalcitrant city with a large army, and the stubborn resistance of the Assisians was finally overcome.

Three years later (1177) Frederick entered the city in person, surrounded by the dazzling pomp of a huge retinue. It was shortly before Christmas. The young emperor had just come from Milan, where he had brutally cast aside the offer of subjection of the city, although the citizens had implored his forgiveness with ropes around their necks. Arrived at Assisi, Frederick mounted the Rocca Maggiore (Big Rock), on which was situated the mighty, towering castle. He remained there about twenty days in order to receive the homage of the feudal lords of the neighborhood and to grant them various concessions.

As his representative in Assisi Frederick appointed the Suabian Konrad of Urslingen, called Lützenhart after his birthplace, but more appropriately "Fly-in-the-brain" (*mosca in cervello*) by the Assisians on account of his stubbornness. He had himself proclaimed Duke of Spoleto and Count of Assisi. From his residence on the Rocca Maggiore he could dominate the entire surrounding country and force full allegiance to the emperor and the feudal lords. In particular, the haughty castle on the Rock was to deter the Assisians from any attempt to free themselves and put their city under the political rule of the pope, who claimed Umbria as one of the jewels in the crown of the papal sovereignty. How secure the Ghibellines felt themselves in this stronghold is evident from the fact that the heir to Frederick's throne, who was a minor and later was to become Frederick II, was entrusted without hesitation to the care of Konrad on the Rocca Maggiore. It is said that the four-year-old prince was baptized with a great display of pomp in the Church of San Rufino, the same church in which Francis also received the sacrament of rebirth.

The hopes which the emperor and with him the whole empire had placed in Assisi were rudely shattered. The fury of the Assisians against the alien usurper increased here as elsewhere from day to day. It exploded like an electrical storm when Barbarossa's successor, Henry VI, died suddenly in September, 1197. The news of his death was the trumpet call to all Italy to rise up against the Ghibelline party. In the beginning of the following year Pope Celestine III also died and was followed by the young and energetic Pope Innocent III. The latter advanced his claims to the duchy of Spoleto, including Assisi, without delay. Fearing the papal army, Konrad of Lützenhart went to Narni in April, 1198, and there surrendered his rule into the hands of the pope.

He had hardly turned his back on Assisi when the storm broke loose with unbridled fury. The townspeople arose, besieged the Rocca Maggiore, overcame the garrison, and razed the mighty fortress. Young and old took part with such fury in the work of destruction that only the foundations and the lower parts of the walls remained.* The burning resentment of the people then turned against the castles of the feudal lords. No tower, no building, no wall was spared. When the twelfth century was drawing to its close, the power of the emperor and the domination of the feudal lords in and around Assisi was broken; the civic republic had been established, the independence of Assisi as a free city had been secured.

It was the merchants who had taken over the leadership in the rebellion. As in other Italian cities, this guild stood at the head of the political revolution. And no wonder. Not only did the most distinguished and the wealthiest citizens belong to it, they also suffered the most at the hands of the lords, who, breaking out of their castles, blocked the highways, exacted bridge and road tolls, and often robbed the merchants at the point of the sword. Peter Bernardone, no doubt, had a very prominent part in the overthrow of the Ghibelline power and in the creation of the new civic constitution; the chronicler, Marianus, calls him outright "the benefactor and administrator of the republic" (*reipublicae benefactor et provisor*).[2] Undoubtedly, Francis also, who at the time was between sixteen and eighteen years of age, took part in the war for the liberation of his native city and with the rest of the inhabitants joyously acclaimed the new republic.

But their joy was of short duration. The humbled barons turned to the neighboring city of Perugia and there acquired citizenship.** Perugia had always been the bitter rival of Assisi. The two cities

---

* The Rocca Maggiore was restored by Albernoz in 1365. The new building arose on the remnants of the old castle which even today can be recognized. For further details see A. Brizzi: *Della Rocca di Assisi*, p. 35 f.

** Fortini, 71 f., makes known the names of the renegades as found in the Assisian archives and also the wording of the agreement reached between them and Perugia. The following details of the war between Assisi and Perugia are likewise based on the historical records unearthed by Fortini for the first time.

constantly vied with one another for territory, commerce, wealth, for their independence. Each one sought to strengthen its position by treaties as well as by conquests and thus to beat down its enemy.

Of greatest moment was the war which Perugia opened in 1200 and which, with several interruptions, lasted for ten years. It was waged under the pretense of protecting the renegade Assisian nobles in their alleged rights. Both sides threw every effort into readying arms and gear for the war. On the side of Assisi were the towns Nocera, Bevagna, Rosciano, and Bastia, which were either subject to Assisi or allied with it. The foot soldiers were recruited from among the workmen and lower-class citizens, while the knights and wealthy townspeople, who were able to furnish their own horses and gear, formed the mounted troops. The son of the rich merchant, Peter Bernardone, naturally belonged to the latter. With banners astream and amid the loud pealing of all the bells of Assisi the mounted soldiers, the archers, and the supply troops marched off to war.

The decisive battle took place in the late fall of the year 1202, somewhere between Collestrada and Ponte San Giovanni, on the road which today still leads from Assisi to Perugia.[3] Although the Assisians performed miracles of valor, they succumbed to the might of the enemy. Boniface of Verona describes in lurid colors the terrible carnage, the flight of the Assisians, the terror and grief which in consequence swept over the city:

Planctus ubique sonat; alii planguntque parentes.
Hac etiam natos et luctus ubique nepotum
Funditur. . . .

Everywhere the cry of mourning; here for parents,
There for sons, elsewhere for nephews. . . .
The battlefield is strewn with dead. . . .
Nowhere a foot joined to hand, nor the rump with the head.
Instead of eyes, gaping holes. . . .
Blood runs in streams, so that the Tescio overflows its banks. . . .
"O Assisians," he cries out, "what a day of misfortune, what an hour of dismal fate. . . . That was the most ruinous defeat which the Perugians ever inflicted on their enemies."[4]

Thomas of Celano and the Three Companions also report this

fatal blood bath and add that many foot soldiers and knights were carried off to Perugia as prisoners. Among them was Francis.[5]

What that implied can hardly be imagined today. The penalty of imprisonment was unbelievably harsh, and the political as well as the military prisoners were treated with barbaric severity. One shrinks in horror at the mere mention of the cruelties inflicted. The prisoners were subjected to torture, loaded down with chains, locked in deep dungeons. In Assisi, Spoleto, Foligno, Terni, Narni, and elsewhere they were pulled up and down on gallows until the thickest kind of ropes broke. In Parma, they were chained to walls in the open so that they remained exposed to the severities of the weather in summer and winter. In Forlì, they were shod with iron, like horses. In Città di Castello they were tied to the tail of a donkey, dragged to the place of execution, and impaled with the head downward. In Milan, their hands were bound behind their backs, and they were then wrapped in bundles of straw and set afire. In Cremona, they were forced to place their food among the piled-up corpses of their fallen comrades, until they were able to pay the poll tax for the dead.[6] In Perugia, there is found to this day a street named "Cage Street" (*Via della Gabbia*). It received this name because an iron cage was suspended over it in which prisoners were locked up and left to die of hunger. But even if they did escape such extreme penalties, the prisoners were chained with irons, penned together in narrow and filthy dungeons, and subjected to indescribable hardships and privations.[7]

The son of Peter Bernardone was not, indeed, placed among the common soldiers. His aristocratic bearing and superior equipment entitled him to be classed with the knights.[8] But these, too, were made to endure bitter sufferings. In later years Francis himself often thought back with horror of the tortures inflicted on him at the time by the Perugians. Thomas of Celano relates that at the mere thought of them he remarked to his companions with a trembling voice: "The people of Perugia have done great evils to their neighbors."[9] Gradually even the strongest and bravest of his fellow prisoners grew despondent. They moaned over their fate and thereby made their lives all the more unbearable.[10]

Only Francis would not allow his spirits to be dampened, although the hardships of the prison must have been doubly agonizing to a nature as delicate as his. He preserved his innate cheerfulness, remained serene and untroubled, and even joked about his chains, so that his companions in misery were seized with wonder. Some even remarked that he must be losing his mind. Francis accepted this jestingly and said: "You do not know why I am so merry. I shall yet be revered throughout the whole world."* With these words he broke into joyous laughter.

In this way Francis exerted a wholesome influence upon his comrades. He was like a sun radiating warmth and light in the dark dungeon. He raised the spirits of the others and dispelled the poisonous air of their quarrelsomeness and discontent. He took special interest in one of the imprisoned knights who was avoided by the rest on account of his arrogance and his unsociable ways. Only Francis associated with him. He bore his evil nature with indestructible patience, helped him to correct his faults, and succeeded in reconciling him with his companions.[11]

Everything in this squire is of a chivalrous character. It was chivalry that prompted him to take up arms for his native city; his merry disposition, his "gay science" amid the squalor and tortures of the dungeon was true chivalry; a true mark of his knightliness was his absolute conviction that he would in future perform great deeds of valor and gain wide renown; truly knightly was his conduct toward his fellow captives and especially his gentleness and his generous forbearance toward the ill-tempered knight. From the crown of his head to the sole of his feet he was wholly a nobleman, to whom was lacking only the formal elevation to knighthood.

---

* Socii, 4. Celano, II, 4, has him say: "I shall yet be revered as a saint throughout the whole world." (*Adhuc sanctus adorabor per saeculum totum.*) Celano, no doubt, added the word "saint" of his own accord. Francis evidently did not think at the time of becoming a saint, much less of being revered as one; but he did hope to become a great prince and gain world-wide renown.

CHAPTER FOUR

For Liege Lord or Vassal?

THE winter passed. Gentle spring held sway for a time and left. The heat of summer burned its way into the dungeon. In endless monotony the days of imprisonment dragged on. The last ray of hope for peace between Perugia and Assisi vanished; in fact, for a whole year both cities had been making preparations for a new campaign. Assisi vowed to avenge its defeat, to punish the renegade nobles, and to regain the lost territory, even to extend it as far as Perugia. On the other hand Perugia made a solemn promise to the renegades not to make a treaty or a truce with Assisi until it had been completely crushed and until full reparation had been made for all damage inflicted. Naturally there was no possibility of repatriating the prisoners under these conditions.

In the meantime Francis had become very ill. In spite of the high spirits in which he had borne his imprisonment, the lack of exercise, of light and air, as well as the other privations had sapped his strength. As a result he was enrolled by the prison keeper in the "Congregation and Company of Sick Prisoners." These could regain their freedom by the payment of money on the part of relatives.[1] Peter Bernardone, the rich merchant, paid the ransom and brought his stricken son home. This was toward the end of the year of 1203, about a year after the calamitous day of Collestrada.*

---

* The Three Companions state definitely (4): "After the end of a year, peace having been made between the aforementioned cities, Francis returned to Assisi with his fellow-prisoners." Heretofore the biographers of the saint assumed accordingly that peace was made between Assisi and Perugia in 1203. However, the documents presented by Fortini, 87–95, prove incontestably that a state of war continued

The illness of Francis had proved very stubborn and its effects lasted during the entire following winter. It was only in the spring of 1204 that he felt his strength slowly returning.* After a while, enough improvement had set in to allow him to walk around in the house with the help of a cane, and even to venture outside. It was only now that it became evident what a deep, spiritual change had come over him. The fertile fields, the lovely vineyards, all the charming countryside lying in the dazzling splendor of the sun, all this earthly beauty which before had so charmed him now left him unmoved. He could not understand how he could have found such pleasure in these things before. Everything had become so different, simply because he himself was no longer the same. Even during his imprisonment he had become thoughtful and now his illness accentuated his seriousness of thought and outlook. His gradual recovery gave him time to realize fully the folly of his former youthful conduct. That God's providence had used his illness to set his feet on another road, of this he was not yet aware. Yet he was seized with a feeling of remorse for his past frivolous life and of contempt for the things which he had before so much admired and sought after.

However, the critical state of his native city probably weighed more heavily on him than the personal trials which he had endured. Assisi was at war with the Church. Since April of 1198 Innocent III had demanded in vain that the city return to the papal sovereignty together with the duchy of Spoleto. The Assisians were determined not to submit to the political rule of the Pope for the reason that their archenemy, Perugia, had joined the Papal states and was enjoying the Pope's special favor.[2] Admonitions, threats, promises were to no avail.[3] The leaders of the rebellion were ex-

---

between these cities without interruption until 1205. The treaty of peace was signed on August 31, of that year, but hostilities soon broke out again and ended only in 1209. That Francis was released from prison while war was still being waged can be explained only by assuming that Bernardone paid a ransom for his ailing son.

* This date may be assumed from Celano, I, 3. Francis had returned from Perugia before the end of 1203. The illness he contracted in prison was a long one (diu infirmitate attritus) and by the time his health was on the mend the fields and vineyards were again in full bloom (pulchritudo agrorum, vinearum amoenitas). Evidently the winter of 1203–1204 lay between.

communicated by the pope.[4] In answer to this, one of the leaders, Girardo di Giliberto, was elected chief magistrate of the city in 1202.* In retaliation the pope placed the city under interdict. This was in the beginning of the year 1203. The churches remained closed, the bells mute, the sacraments were administered only to the dying, the Church seemed to live only for the dead.[5] The bitter resentment of the Assisians now gave way to the gloom of despair. This was the state in which Francis found his beloved city on his return from Perugia and during his lingering, tedious illness.

When the interdict was finally lifted on June 6, 1203, the war with Perugia flamed up anew and with greater vehemence than ever. Francis, of course, could no longer take part in it. Evidently he had been given his freedom only under the condition that he would never again draw his sword against the neighboring city. The distress of his own native city rested all the more heavily on him. Commerce, industry, and agriculture were prostrate. Poverty increased from day to day. Some of the citizens were forced to sell their fields and vineyards in order to appease their hunger. Even noblemen could be seen begging in the streets in ragged clothing. The city was unable to pay the wages of the knights and mercenaries who had been hired from other places. Perugia, too, was exhausted. And so on August 31, 1205, Perugia and Assisi finally agreed to a peace which was acceptable to both, a peace, however, which was to be of very short duration.[6]

The foreign knights employed by Assisi now sought other battlefields, and more than one Assisian who had become accustomed to soldiering was tempted to accompany them. Francis himself was straining for the opportunity of going forth as the squire of some brave knight and ultimately of reaching the rank of knighthood himself. Even though many of his youthful dreams had vanished since the eventful day of Collestrada, and even though his exuberant enthusiasm for the "gay science" had given way to more sober reflec-

---

* The list of the consuls of the city republic is found in Fortini, 386. According to this list Girardo di Giliberto was replaced as consul already in June, 1203. However, he appears as consul in a document dated December 29, 1203 (Fortini, 436). Girardo, no doubt, commanded the Assisian forces at the battle of Collestrada.

tion, yet he never renounced his great plans and high purposes. Even when pining in the darkness and horrors of the dungeon he had spoken triumphantly of his future greatness. Ever since he had gained his freedom and during his long convalescence, his gaze had turned southward, where success seemed to beckon.

The Hohenstaufen emperor, Henry VI, had incorporated the kingdom of Sicily and Apulia, which were fiefs of the Church, into his empire. But after his death at Messina, in 1197, his widow Constance not only acknowledged the papal suzerainty, but appointed Innocent III as the guardian of the three-year-old successor, Frederick II, and thereby also as regent of the kingdom. While the pope was endeavoring to defend his fiefs and to protect the rights of his ward, the Lord High Steward Markwald of Anweiler with the aid of a large army sought to usurp the regency over southern Italy. For a time victory perched on one banner and then on the other, until Innocent III entrusted his cause to Count Walter of Brienne, Duke of Tarent and Lecce. One victory after another now followed the papal standards.[7] The romantic soul of the Italian people now saw in the hero of Brienne their liberator from alien usurpers and tyrants. All acclaimed him jubilantly. The troubadours sang the fame of his exploits from city to city and summoned all to join his victorious colors. A storm of enthusiasm swept over the land. Bold adventurers, brave knights, soldiers craving for action streamed together from all sides. All hoped to gain fame and distinction, money and booty, land and titles by joining the ranks of the renowned leader. Now, if ever, the fulfillment of his grand dreams of becoming a knight and a prince appeared within the reach of Francis.

Suddenly the crushing news arrived that the hero of Brienne had died. On June 11, 1205, while besieging the castle of Sarno, he was treacherously set upon by the German robber, Baron Diutpold, and three days later he succumbed to the wounds suffered in the attack.*

---

* *Gesta Innocentii III*, cap. XXXVIII, col. 67; Luchaire, *loc. cit.*, 191. Since Assisi was still at war with Perugia, the departure of Francis must have been delayed until peace was made on August 31, 1205. But it must have taken place shortly after this date, otherwise there would not have been sufficient time for the events which occurred in the life of Francis up to his final conversion.

His army, however, continued the fight and was being constantly swelled by enlistments from northern and central Italy. In Assisi, too, a certain nobleman was preparing to journey to Apulia. Francis quickly determined to follow this former comrade-in-arms of Collestrada, who had also been a fellow prisoner at Perugia, as a squire and to win for himself the rank of a knight fighting at the side of Count Gentile of Manupello.* This count was the brother of the royal chancellor of Sicily and Apulia. He had distinguished himself in the victorious battle of Palermo against Markwald of Anweiler and enjoyed such prestige that many thought he himself had ambitions for the royal crown of southern Italy.[8]

At any rate Francis was convinced that by fighting in the ranks of the count and by performing great deeds of valor he could merit promotion to the rank of knighthood. He therefore provided himself with a horse and the necessary arms and accouterment as well as sumptuous garments, so that he could present a thoroughly knightly appearance.[9] He was far more interested, however, in displaying the knightly quality of munificence, in which he was superior to his noble fellow citizen.[10] The day before his departure he met a knight who was so badly in need of clothing that he could not take part in the expedition to Apulia. Francis did not hesitate a moment. "For love of Christ," he said, taking off the costly garments he was wearing for the first time, and gave them to his comrade-in-arms.[11]

A few hours later he lay down to sleep. It was his last night under his father's roof. But sleep refused to come. A thousand daring plans stormed in his soul. Wild battle scenes were conjured up by his feverish fancy. His pulses raced in anticipation of his approaching departure. Finally he fell asleep. However, all the pictures and

---

* Socii, 5. While most biographers from Sabatier, *Vie de S. François* (1904), p. 19, to Fortini, *loc. cit.,* 99, repeat that Francis journeyed with a Count Gentile, the Three Companions state explicitly that he traveled to Apulia with an unknown nobleman of Assisi, in order "to be made a knight there by a certain Count by the name of Gentile." Up till now it had been believed that this count could not be identified further, because there was a great number of men bearing the name Gentile. However, in the battles for the kingdom of Sicily, to which the duchy of Apulia belonged, there is found only one bearer of this name, and that is Count Gentile of Manupello. This leaves hardly a doubt that Francis hoped to be made a knight by him in the near future.

scenes which had filled his mind previously, now entered his dreams with greater intensity and vividness. An illustrious lord led him into a spacious and beautiful palace rising majestically from the roadside. The exterior of the palace was covered with heraldic bearings, the interior walls were resplendent with armor and weapons which were marked with the sign of the cross. In the assembly hall a wondrously lovely maiden awaited her bridegroom. Filled with elation Francis inquired for whom all this splendor and glory was reserved. "For you," a voice answered, "and for your knights."[12]

Now everything seemed clear. He would be made a knight in Apulia. From there he would journey to the Holy Land, like so many other knights of his day, and wearing the red cross on his ensign and his armor, he would battle for the deliverance of the holy places. He would return from the Crusade with a high rank of nobility and followed by a large retinue enter his princely castle at the side of a noble and gracious wife.

He awoke suddenly, made his farewells to the family, swung himself upon his mount, and gaily rode off into the morning. The townspeople, who wondered at his impetuous haste, received the explanation: "I know that I am going to be a great prince."[13] He galloped away, his heart swelling with elation and enthusiasm over the expected honors and riches. After a hard day's ride he arrived tired and spent at Spoleto, where he immediately engaged quarters for the night.

It was here that he had another apparition in his half sleep. He found himself engaged in a strange colloquy with a noble lord, who inquired where he was going and what was the purpose of his journey. Francis replied that he was journeying to Apulia with a countryman in order to win for himself a knight's sword, fame, and riches. "Who can do you more good, the master or the servant?" the apparition asked. Francis answered: "The master." "Why then do you forsake the master for the servant and the lord for the vassal?" Francis again replied: "What wilt Thou, Lord, that I do?" "Return to your country, for the revelation which you have just received, shall find spiritual fulfillment through Me."[14]

He awoke and began to reflect on the remarkable words he had heard. No doubt remained: in the language of chivalry "master" meant nothing else than "Supreme Liege Lord," "Most High Emperor of heaven," and "servant" on the other hand meant "human liege man," "feudal vassal." The strange message was neither an illusion nor the product of his imagination. In his state of mind, which was wholly absorbed with mundane greatness and earthly riches, Francis could not have had hallucinations of a spiritual and superworldly nature. For hallucinations are only the mirror of the things with which the mind of the victim is occupied. They are always directly related to his fixed ideas. They produce only such seemingly real images as he has been nurturing in the inner recesses of his soul.

Francis was fully convinced that he was called by God to a wholly different kind of knighthood than the one of which he had dreamed. He never lost this certainty during the rest of his life — an incontestable proof, too, that it was not a mere dream — just as he had the certainty at this moment of the truth of the words he had heard. This brought about a complete change in him. Just as he had before experienced the greatest elation when expecting the realization of his fondest earthly hopes, so he now could hardly master his joy over the promised spiritual riches. Sleep had now fled completely. At the first graying of dawn he leaped from his couch, saddled his horse, and rode back to Assisi.

Filled with a holy enthusiasm he surrendered wholly to the divine will, which, though not recognized by him, had been leading him for a long time. Firmly determined to follow the voice, he resolved to exchange, as Celano says, the carnal weapons for the spiritual, the worldly fame of a knight for the fame of spiritual knight-errantry.[15] As the squire of an earthly vassal he had gone forth from Assisi, now he turned his face again to his native city, heeding the call of the "Emperor of heaven" to become His "servant" and knight.

CHAPTER FIVE

Francis Is Knighted by Christ

THE news of the sudden return of Francis spread like wildfire from mouth to mouth. The townspeople sought in vain to solve this puzzle, which was all the more baffling because Francis showed such great spirit of elation in spite of the occurrence. To everyone who ventured to penetrate the secret of his odd behavior Francis gave the same answer: "I shall not go to Apulia, yet I shall become a great prince."[1]

However, in his own mind he was by no means clear regarding his future course of action. Only one thing was certain: he was to serve the Lord as a spiritual knight. But just what this service implied, what God wanted him to do, and how he was to accomplish this — all this was still wrapped in mystery. Yet, surely, the Lord who had called him to His service would lead him onward. For the time being, his work was to adapt himself to his new calling, to become a faithful liege man of the Lord, and thus prepare himself for the spiritual knighthood.

However, his former companions were to cause some difficulties. They were aware that he had abandoned his journey to Apulia but not his high-flown plans. They therefore took it for granted that he would continue his former gay life with them. No matter how much he remonstrated, they again chose him as their *podestá* and kept urging him to prepare another of his joyous feasts.

Francis yielded only once, but merely because he did not want to appear niggardly. He had a sumptuous feast prepared, called his old comrades together, and played the host with truly chivalrous amiability. During the whole evening, however, he seemed lost in thought. After the company had indulged in food and drink far beyond the limits of necessity, they roamed as usual through the streets of the city and filled the night with the sound of merry song. Francis followed them, holding in his right hand a staff, the scepter of the King of Youth. Gradually, however, his feet began to drag and his steps to falter. Finally he stood still, as if entranced, his heart raised in praise and adoration to God in whom he was now completely lost. Ecstasy flooded his whole being and filled him with such sweet delight that he no longer saw nor heard nor felt anything. As he confessed later, it would have been impossible for him to move an inch at the time, even if he had been cut to pieces.[2]

At that moment his roistering companions turned a street corner and noticed that Francis had remained behind. They shouted to him. To no avail. They ran back to him. No movement. They saw that he seemed to be out of his senses, and some began to reproach him saying that he was no longer the same person since his return from Spoleto. Still no answer, until one of the more daring ones laughingly asked him: "Tell us, Francis, are you in love? Are you thinking of taking a bride?" Francis seemed to awaken and in a lively tone he replied: "Yes, I was thinking of the bride who is to be mine, a bride nobler, richer, and more beautiful than any you have ever seen."

A shout of laughter greeted this statement. What a fanciful dream! And yet Francis had actually met the lady of his heart for the second time. Only this time it was an otherworldly, spiritual, heavenly woman, much nobler, richer, and more charming than the bride which had appeared to him in the dream-vision before his departure for Spoleto.*

That evening he said farewell not only to his former comrades, the sharers of his past frivolities, but to the world in general. Perhaps not completely; for duty and decency advised against a complete break, and after all the last small roots which still held him tied

---

* Cel., I, 7, and Socii, 7, interpret the vision to mean that Francis saw his future Order in the figure of this bride. But at this time Francis had no idea whatsoever of founding an Order.

to worldly trifles had not been wholly loosened. But he made strenuous efforts to break these roots one after the other, to arrive at contempt and renunciation of himself and of all the things which he had formerly held in high esteem and loved so ardently.

He now completely denied himself sensual comforts and pleasures. As often and as long as he could manage it he withdrew from the bustle of business and the clamor of human association in order to spend his time in prayer and reflection. This, however, was done in a way to avoid notice, quietly and unaffectedly. To use the allegory of the Gospel, as a shrewd merchant he wanted to hide the pearl which he had found from prying eyes and quietly make it his own, even at the cost of all his earthly goods.

There was one young man, however, to whom he entrusted his great secret, a friend and companion of about his own age, for whom he cherished a warm affection and whose counsel he frequently sought. To him he opened his heart, telling him that he had found a secret, precious treasure. His friend was overjoyed and waited with tense eagerness for the outcome of the mysterious affair. Day after day he followed Francis whenever the latter went out on his so-called treasure hunt. Beyond the city in an isolated spot there was a cave — perhaps an old Etruscan grave — to which they directed their steps, conversing on the way about the hidden treasure.

When they arrived at the cave the companion had to remain on guard at some distance, while Francis entered the secret retreat. Here he cast himself humbly upon his knees and prayed with all the fervor of his heart to his heavenly Father. With the simplicity and directness of a child he besought the Father to lead him in His infinitely kind providence to the path he was to choose, to help him recognize and to do the divine will. His heart beat feverishly; his cheeks glowed; from his brow drops of sweat mingled with the tears flowing from his eyes and dampened the ground. He suffered unspeakably, because he was at a loss regarding the manner in which he was to put his new calling into action.

A hundred plans were considered, accepted, and again rejected. Not one seemed to lead to the desired goal. Nowhere could he find a clear path, no light came from above to dispel the darkness enshrouding him. And yet within him burned the fierce desire to do even the most difficult things if God so commanded. He was overcome by such a consuming ardor that he had to find relief in sighs and groans. In spite of all he was oppressed by the fear that he might become unfaithful to his calling, no matter how deep his sorrow for his past errors and how firm his resolve to trample under foot all earthly joys and vanities. When he finally returned to his companion after wrestling with God for hours on end, he was so exhausted that he could hardly be recognized.

At last the light broke through the dark clouds of doubt and his future course of action lay clear before him. He had been beseeching the mercy of God in long and fervent prayer when it was revealed to him what he was to do for the time being. From this moment on he was filled with such inexpressible joy that he was almost beside himself. Though he tried to conceal his happiness, yet he unwittingly allowed others to notice the change.

However, his speech was very cautious and mysterious. Just as he had spoken to his young friend about a hidden treasure, so now he spoke to others of his good fortune only in figures of speech and allegories. If they pressed him with the question whether he planned to resume his journey to Apulia, his constant answer was: "By no means; however, I shall perform great and noble deeds here in my own country." Some were of the opinion that he had intentions of marriage and asked him: "Do you intend to bring home a bride, Francis?" To this question he replied gaily as he had before: "Yes, I shall bring home a bride nobler and more beautiful than you have ever seen, a bride who surpasses all in beauty of figure and who excels all in wisdom."[3] It had become clear to him that God had destined holy Lady Poverty to be his bride and life's companion.

He now set about courting this bride in all seriousness. First of all he made the cause of the poor his very own. Until now he had been openhanded toward all needy persons, but from now on he took the poor into his heart of hearts. His alms were more generous and given more joyously. Whenever he met a beggar on the road he gave him whatever money he carried on his person at the time;

if he had none, he gave away his cap or his shoes or other parts of his clothing, just so that the beggar would not be dismissed empty-handed. At times he would withdraw to some lonely spot, take off his shirt, and send the beggar there to retrieve it — *por amore di Dio,* "for the love of God." Nor did he forget the poor, little churches; he bought various articles for them and secretly sent them to poor priests.

Whenever he happened to be eating at home in the absence of his father he nevertheless set places for all the members of the family. If Donna Pica asked why he had set so many loaves of bread on the table, he answered: "I do this so that I might give them as alms to the poor, for I have vowed to give bread to all who ask for it in the name of God." Pica did not interfere, because she loved him more than any of the other children. In fact, she was filled with joy and admiration over the kindheartedness of her son.

But this was not enough for Francis. He wanted to be a real friend to the poor and not only their benefactor. Formerly he had been interested only in gathering his comrades about himself and being their leader in various amusements. He could never bring himself to resist their invitations. As soon as he heard their call, he would leave everything and follow them. If they happened to pass by his home while he was at table with the family, he would eagerly rush out to join them, though he had barely started eating, and though he felt that his conduct was a sore trial for his parents. But now he began to show the same interest and affection for the poor. He took the greatest delight in meeting them, talking with them, and sharing his money and belongings with them.

But he took still greater delight in appearing like them. In fact his one great desire was now to become one of them. The grace of God had wrought such a change in him that he had but one wish — to live in some strange city unknown to all, to exchange his costly garments for the rags of a beggar and test his love for his Lady Poverty by begging alms like the poor, for the love of God.

It was this desire which determined him to make a pilgrimage to Rome, to the tomb of the Apostles, who likewise chose to become poor for Christ's sake. After arriving in the Eternal City, he entered the church of St. Peter. He saw with a deep hurt that the offerings of the faithful were very sparing, and he said to himself: "The prince of the Apostles, St. Peter, surely deserves to be honored in a princely manner. Why then do they make such beggarly offerings to the church in which his body rests?" With these words he took a purse filled with money from his waistband and threw it with a loud crash into the almsbox at the altar, so that all those present marveled at his lavishness.

After satisfying his devotion he stepped out on the open place before the church which the beggars called the "paradise," because it was there that they usually gleaned a rich harvest of alms. Francis found himself immediately surrounded by a throng of mendicants. He gave alms to each one, sat down gaily among them and ate so heartily with them that he seemed to be one of their number. Then he unobtrusively borrowed the ragged clothing of one of the beggars, gave him his rich costume in exchange, and began to beg alms in French on the steps of the church. He had only a smattering of this language, yet he preferred to use it because it was the language of the troubadours and of chivalry. After playing the role of a beggar for some time, and rejoicing in the knowledge that he had played his role well, he took off the beggar's rags, put on his own clothing, and returned to Assisi. He reveled in the joyful thought that he had put himself on equal footing with the penniless, the poor whom his Lord Jesus Christ had so loved and championed.

He longed to join their company immediately in his native city. Yet he dared not take this step because he felt that he was still under obligation to his family. But he prayed all the harder that God might lead him on the path of poverty. He also consulted Bishop Guido Secundi several times, hoping that his doubts might be removed and the way made clear how to carry out his project. But no one else was allowed to share his secret. In his day it was unheard of to live in absolute poverty, and it was just this sublime ideal which he longed to attain above all things of this world. He was determined to live and to die in complete, absolute poverty.[4]

But before he was to achieve this great and final victory over the world, he had to learn to gain a complete victory over himself. One day, while praying with great ardor to the Crucified, he received the behest: "Francis, you must loath and despise everything which you have hitherto loved and pursued in a fleshly manner, if you wish to do My will. Once you have begun to do this in all seriousness everything will become bitter and insufferable which formerly appeared sweet and delectable, and everything which formerly stirred fear and loathing in you will cause you great sweetness and unspeakable delight."[5]

Francis received this behest with great joy and determination, though he surmised what these words meant. As long as he could remember, he had been seized with unconquerable loathing at the sight of ugly people and especially of lepers. The mere thought of these poor wretches made him shudder. Their nearness was so unbearable to him that, as he confessed later, he used to turn away and hold his nose when he came in sight of a leper house, even if it was several miles away. Not that he was insensible to their misery; his repugnance was stronger than his compassion. If he happened to meet a leper unexpectedly, he would have someone else offer the alms for him, and then hastily depart.[6]

That, however, was not in harmony with chivalry, with his calling to the knighthood of Christ. Jesus had made the lepers the special object of his love; of Him it had been written: "He has borne our infirmities and carried our sorrows: and we have thought him as it were a leper, and as one struck by God and afflicted" (Isa. 53:4). Indeed, the Church and the Middle Ages saw in the lepers Christ Himself, who like them had been driven from human society, had been looked upon as an outcast, as the Man of sorrows. Anyone, then, who was called to serve Christ as His knight, would have to conquer his aversion to the lepers and learn to love them.

With this thought troubling his mind Francis one day was riding over the plain below Assisi. A deep sense of shame had overpowered him. Without any doubt the Lord demanded of him to take a resolute stand regarding the lepers by an act of heroic self-conquest. Suddenly, as he was turning a corner in the road, he came face to face with one of these pitiable creatures. The unexpected meeting made him cringe with fear and abhorrence. But immediately he

remembered the Lord's injunction to conquer himself if he wished
to become a knight of Christ. Hastily gathering his courage he
leaped from his horse, handed a coin to the leper, and embraced and
kissed him. Again mounting his horse he rode off joyously. When
he looked back again over the wide and open plain the leper was
nowhere to be seen. Francis was filled with great wonder and joy,
knowing that the Saviour had deigned to appear to him in the
person of the leper. He began to sing the praises of God, firmly
resolved to deny himself still more in future and to seek only the
closest union with his Most High Lord.[7]

He returned home, filled his purse with money, and hastened to
the lazaretto of San Salvatore delle Pareti, near Assisi. There he
gathered all the lepers, gave alms to each and kissed their hands.
From this day on he also visited other leper colonies frequently,
giving alms to the sufferers and rendering such loving services as
only a mother would render her sick child. All this because he saw
in every leper the crucified Saviour.[8]

Joined to this heroism of self-conquest and ministering love was
a constantly increasing union with God. Accompanied by his young
friend, he continued his visits to the cave of Subasio, ostensibly to
dig for treasure. At other times he visited lonely churches and
chapels in and around Assisi, of which there were about a hundred
in his day.*

There was one church, however, which he favored and to which
he directed his steps most often, the little church of San Damiano. It
was situated some distance from the eastern city wall, in the middle
of a cypress and olive grove. The little sanctuary was at the time
almost in ruins and abandoned by everybody. Only one, a poor
priest named Don Pietro according to tradition, gave it what little
attention and care he could. It harbored one treasure — a venerable
old crucifix, which the Poor Ladies of St. Damian's were soon to
make their own. Later on they took it to Santa Chiara as a precious
relic, and it is venerated there to this day. The figure of the Cruci-

---

* Fortini, 384 f., enumerates all that existed in Francis' time with the dates on
which they are mentioned for the first time in the archives of the city and of
the Cathedral of San Rufino. Many of these are still standing today.

fied, in the Byzantine style, has a very touching expression. With a gentle yet serious and majestic look the Saviour seems to penetrate to the very depths of one's soul, at the same time inviting one to follow Him. Here at St. Damian's Francis delighted to pray, and here occurred that astounding miracle which was to be decisive for his whole future life.

One day, while on his knees before the image of the Crucified, he entreated the Saviour with great urgency for light and strength. Suddenly he heard the words clearly and distinctly: "Francis, do you not see that My house is falling into ruins? Make haste and rebuild it!" These words were spoken three times with unutterable sweetness and with increasing urgency. Feelings of joy as well as of awe rioted in the heart of Francis. Trembling he gave answer: "Gladly will I do so, my Lord." He was so deeply stirred that he almost fell into ecstasy, but at the same time he also received an interior enlightenment making it clear to him without a shadow of a doubt: it was the Crucified Himself who had spoken to him.

He gave fervent thanks for the grace received and left the little church. Coming out into the open he found himself face to face with Don Pietro, who was sitting on a bench beside the sanctuary. He gave the priest whatever money he had at the time and said to him: "I beseech you, my lord, to buy oil for a lamp which is to burn constantly before the crucifix. As soon as this amount is used up, I will attend further to it so that the holy image will always remain honored." Then he hastened away with the resolve to take the necessary steps to carry out the command of the Crucified.[9]

But did not this command to rebuild the church stand in the way of his plans for a knightly career? On the contrary, the figure of the Crucified of St. Damian's spoke the language of chivalry.[10] In the *chansons de geste* of chivalric literature the construction and repair of churches and cloisters often appears as a duty of honor incumbent on the heroes of these epic poems. They carry sand, mix the mortar, cut the stones, build the walls, in other words, they *work* as common laborers and craftsmen. Girard of Roussillon, Renaud of Montauban, and many other heroes devoted a part of their lives to the building and repairing of God's temples. Thus the mandate given by the figure of the Crucified could be understood by Francis in no other way than that he was being raised to the knighthood of the cross.

It was essential that Christ Himself spoke from the crucifix. Even the lay squires were knighted in the sign of the cross.[11] During the Crusades it was the supreme duty of the knight to be "Christ's servant and warrior," "a liege man of Christ, who for us was crucified," a vassal of Christ faithful unto death.[12] The members of the religious military Orders were designated with all the more reason as "cowarriors and comrades-in-arms of Christ." St. Bernard of Clairvaux reminded them that while they had chosen the vocation of soldiers as secular knights, as religious knights they were to cultivate a saintly deportment, protect the poor and the churches, and give their lives for Christ.*

Francis, however, had been consecrated a knight by the sovereign Liege Lord Himself. In the well-known language of chivalry the behest given by the Crucified meant definitely that he was enrolled among the liege men (ministerials), among that class of free noblemen who spent their days at the court and in the palace of the king as honor guards. The miraculous occurrence at St. Damian's had made the deepest impression on him and had changed him completely. There was no longer any thought of that worldly knight-

---

* In the oldest rule of a military Order, that of the Knights Templar, we already read this exhortation of St. Bernard of Clairvaux: "Preface of the Rule of the Co-warriors of Christ. . . . We therefore exhort you, who until now have chosen the worldly army not for Christ's sake, but solely for human favor, that you hasten to join the company of those whom God has chosen from the mass of the damned and has made defenders of Holy Church by His gratuitous mercy. Above all things, however, no matter who you are, O knight of Christ, choose such a holy deportment . . . that by observing it purely and constantly you may merit to be numbered among those knights who have given their lives for Christ." (*Praefatio Regulae Commilitonum Christi . . . Hortamur itaque vos, qui usque nunc miliciam saecularem, in qua Christus non fuit causa, sed solo humano favore amplexi estis, quatenus horum unitati, quos Deus ex massa perditionis elegit et ad defensionem sanctae ecclesiae gratuita pietate composuit, vos sociandos perhenniter festinetis. Ante omnia autem, quicumque es, O Christi miles, tam sanctam conversationem eligens . . . ut, si pure et perseveranter observetur, inter militares, qui pro Christo animas suas dederunt, sortem obtinere mereberis.*) Holstenius, *Codex Regularum* II, 131; G. Schnürer, *Die ursprüngliche Templerregel* (Freiburg i. Br., 1903), p. 130.

hood which so long had been the stuff of his dreams and of his desires. He was unspeakably happy — and was to remain so all his life — that he had been made the knight-errant, the "liege man of Christ who for us was crucified."

CHAPTER SIX

Francis Courts the Lady Poverty

THERE was still one thing which Francis, the knight of Christ, lacked — the noble bride of whom he had spoken and dreamed so long.

Chivalry was simply unthinkable without the cult of woman. Whether espoused to him in Christian wedlock, courted by him with passionate love, or at least looked upon as a symbol of things spiritual and exalted, the knight could never be without the lady of his heart. The woman whom he was allowed to call his "lady" gave him a "prize," an expression of her special favor which singled him out from all others. In the heat of a tilting contest she spurred on his bravery. "God help me, that is truly a brave knight!" the lady would exclaim when the passage-of-arms reached its climax. "May God love me as I love her!" the knight replied. No tournament was complete without a final joust in honor of the ladies. In strange lands, in the heat and din of battle, in the comparative peace of camp life the knight kept the memory of his ladylove sacred in order to remain brave and true and to guard against any ignoble action. To pay homage to her, to defend her, to serve at her side, was just as much a sacred duty to him as unfailing fealty to his liege lord.

This chivalrous cult of woman could not, of course, always remain on this high plane. Many a brave warrior fell victim to the "eternally feminine." This weakness did not appear in the heroes of the *Song of Roland,* nor in the heroes of the oldest epics of chivalry. The romances of the Round Table, however, pay heavy tribute to lighthearted gallantry. The poetry of the Provençal troubadours often reveled in erotic affairs, not seldom even in the most ardent affairs of passion. This was an indication that knighthood had already become degenerate. The love of the genuine Christian knight was directed to woman in the ideal sense of the word, to innocence and purity, to graciousness and charm and loving helpfulness, to the mother in woman, to the feminine ideal in its truest form.

Francis knew this ideal and from the beginning included it in his plans. Just as he always felt and gave the assurance that he would become a famous prince, so he always dreamed also of a noble bride. When he was about to set forth on his journey to Apulia, he saw in a vision his future princely palace and also the wondrous maiden at whose side he was to enter it. After his return to Assisi he explained to his youthful companions that he had, indeed, abandoned his plan of journeying to the South, but not his plan of becoming a prince, and still less his dream of an illustrious bride, richer, more noble, and more beautiful than anyone could imagine. Even during the days when he was torn between various agonizing uncertainties regarding the course of action God wished him to take, the assurance never left him that his destined bride would excel all noble women in charm and beauty as well as in wisdom. There is no doubt that at this time his thoughts were of some human person, just as the knighthood to which he aspired then included the worldly splendor of a prince.

The decisive change came in that night at Spoleto when the Lord said to him: "Return to your home, for the vision which you have had shall find a spiritual fulfilment through Me." No doubt this was meant not only of his dreams of becoming a prince but also of winning a bride of noble estate. Francis wondered. Was it not perhaps the poverty of Christ which God had destined to be his spiritual bride?

From the earliest days of his youth he had fostered, as we have seen, the Christian viewpoint of seeing Christ in the persons of the poor; he had followed the norms of chivalry in being openhanded toward them. Ever since he had heard the Lord tell him that his dreams and plans for the future had a spiritual significance, he had felt an ever stronger and more ardent affection for the dispossessed and the needy. He made their cause his own, longed to be like them, and on one occasion he had tested himself by soliciting alms like a beggar. At that time he was jubilant because he had succeeded, and now he was determined to make more frequent invasions into the realm of poverty. There existed for him no contradiction between poverty for the love of Christ and the noble bride who had been promised him. In fact, it was his chivalrous nature which impelled him to choose poverty for the very reason that it was disparaged, despised, shunned. And because he possessed a pronounced flair for vitalizing and personifying all lifeless and abstract things, he also personalized the spirit and the virtue of poverty and looked on it as a living, concrete, personal being, as "Madonna Povertà."

Then came that momentous hour when he was knighted by Christ at St. Damian's. The Crucified Himself spoke to him and enlisted him for His personal service. Thereby he was clearly destined also for the service of the poor yet royal bride whom the Saviour had chosen for Himself, she who had been faithful to Him from Bethlehem to Golgotha and in whose embrace He had breathed forth His soul on the tree of torture. For Francis, who knew the language of the troubadours so well, there was no longer any mystery. As he was bound to his Lord as a liege man, so also was he bound as a knightly troubadour to Lady Poverty.

Even more. Because this heavenly bride had become widowed and lonely since the death on the cross of her divine Lord, the new knight of Christ, Francis, was to take her as his Lady and Spouse in place of Christ. He was not only to serve her, pay homage to her, and sing her praises with a courtly and chivalrous love, he was also to make himself fully like her by the complete renunciation of all earthly things. However, he was still far from this goal, even though he was attached to his new bride with all his heart. He was still the purse-proud merchant's son who lacked nothing and who could claim a share in his father's business and fortune. He therefore pondered ways and means of ridding himself of everything which stood between him and the noble Lady Poverty.

The solution of this problem did not seem too difficult. It often happened in Assisi as elsewhere that devout persons dedicated themselves and their fortune to a church for the purpose of living only for God and the salvation of their souls. That was the plan of Francis. He resolved to dedicate himself as an oblate to the little Church of St. Damian, that hallowed sanctuary where the Crucified had spoken to him. He would devote all his efforts to restoring the house of God, since this evidently was the mandate given him by Christ. In virtue of this mandate from above he was undoubtedly entitled to possess himself of the necessary means from his father's business. He would gladly renounce all other claims to his father's fortune in order to spend his life as the knightly bridegroom of noble Lady Poverty.

But how was he to carry out this plan? He dared not give even an inkling of his project to his father, who surely would have regarded it as madness on the part of his fanatic son. Some ruse would have to be devised.

Francis bowed low before the figure of the Crucified in the little church of St. Damian where he had been praying and hastened home. The following day he declared that he intended to travel to the market of Foligno. Bernardone was very agreeably surprised! At last his oldest son was again showing some interest in his business! Never had Bernardone agreed to a plan of Francis more readily. Francis signed himself with the cross, saddled his horse, loaded it with bolts of precious cloth, and jogged off for Foligno, the center of Umbrian trade.

At Foligno he sold everything he had brought with him: cloth, horse, saddle, and equipment. Then he began the return journey on foot. It led him past St. Damian's, where he halted, approached Don Pietro, reverently kissed his hand, and offered his purse with the statement that he was giving himself also to the church as an oblate. The priest was speechless. Only a short while ago the young man had made a generous donation, and now he was offering a much larger sum! Would not Pietro Bernardone rise up in anger over this wastefulness of his son? Did Francis wish to cause grave embarrassment to the priest? Did not everyone know his worldly-mindedness, his constant dreaming of gay feasts and grand achievements? Don Pietro was skeptical and refused to take the money.

But Francis was not to be dissuaded. With complete candor and with that childlike trust which he had shown toward the priest from the beginning, he began to tell how God had changed him from a worldling to His knight, and how the Crucified Himself had enlisted him in this very chapel in His service and had commanded him to rebuild it. He wished to begin this work without delay, and all he asked of the reverend Father was that he might remain at St. Damian's as an oblate. Since he had already dedicated himself to the service of God, he would not return to his father's roof anyway, but was determined to lead a life devoted to piety.

All this he said with such fiery conviction and with such inflexible determination that Don Pietro could no longer have any doubt about the truth of his statements. But he feared the anger of Bernardone all the more. Francis, however, pleaded insistently that he be allowed to live in the shadow of the church. Finally Don Pietro assented. Francis was of age and was master of his own future. But the money which Bernardone might claim as his the priest absolutely refused to take. Thereupon Francis threw it into a window niche which opened into the church. Then he thanked Don Pietro humbly for his hospitality and entered the sanctuary to pray.*

Days passed by. In Bernardone's household the return of Francis from Foligno was expected from hour to hour. In vain. Fearing some accident had befallen him, they searched every road and path all the way to Foligno, ten miles distant. At last he was discovered at St. Damian's, where he was busying himself in the church. But

---

* Cel., I, 8. 9; Socii, 16. That Francis really had the intention of becoming an oblate of the little Church is shown conclusively by the words of his first biographer: " . . . (Francis) begged urgently and pleaded with the priest that he would allow him to *abide* with him for the sake of the Lord. The priest finally consented to his *abiding* there. (. . . *orans enixius et deprecans sacerdotem ut eum secum morari pro Domino pateretur. Acquievit tandem sacerdos de mora illius.*)" It is precisely this term *mora, morari* which designated the condition of oblates. The civic statutes of Assisi (Fortini, 149, n. 10) define those as oblates who "have a continuous *abode* at the hostel (*oblatum et oblatam, eiusdem hospitalis ibidem moram continuam habentes*)." Furthermore, Francis soon afterward appeared in the garb of an oblate of St. Damian at the trial instituted by his father.

he could not be moved to return home; he insisted that he had entered the service of the Lord. Bernardone was highly indignant and determined to force the issue. Calling together his friends and neighbors he hastened with them to San Damiano.

Francis heard the thunder of their threats from afar off. And since he was, as the Three Companions remark, still a novice among the knights of Christ, he was not brave enough to meet his enemies face to face. He fled to one of the many caves at the foot of Monte Subasio, one which he had already chosen for this very purpose. The band stormed past without discovering his hiding place. His stay there was known only to Don Pietro and to a loyal and discreet servant of his father's household, who occasionally brought him some food. Now he was alone with God. With fasting and prayer he implored the mercy of his crucified Saviour; he now placed all his trust in Him since he could no longer hope for human help. He fervently begged the Lord to deliver him from the hands of his persecutors so that he might be able to restore the little church of St. Damian as he had been bidden.

He spent a whole month in the solitude of the cave. And however deplorable his condition might seem to be, he was immeasurably happy; the days spent alone here were days of rich grace. He grew stronger in spirit from hour to hour until he finally felt that he had won the victory over himself. He had at last fought his way to the heights of true knightliness. He began to feel ashamed of his fear, or as he now regarded it — his cowardice. Boldly he left the cave, ready to battle and to suffer for the Lord. Carrying the shield of faith and armed with the sword of firm trust in God, he set out for the city. Like his divine Lord and Master he was ready to suffer mistreatment and contempt.

He knew only too well what to expect. He knew the fiery anger of his father. The threats which the latter had uttered a month ago still shrilled in his ears. The servant who had been loyal to him had reported repeatedly that Bernardone's rage was growing in proportion as the sensation increased which was caused by Francis' conduct. Assisi was a small place, just large enough to make the young man's apparent madness the talk of the town. His fellow citizens were of one mind — Francis had become a victim of his eccentricities, he had lost his mind.

His whole appearance at this moment confirmed this verdict. The gay young blade and former *podestá* of "golden youth" presented such an uncouth appearance that he was hardly recognizable. His long concealment in the dark cave, the constant castigation of the flesh, hunger and privation had wrought a great change in him. His clothes were neglected, his figure gaunt, his face pale, and his cheeks sunken. The street urchins took him for one of the mentally deranged people who wandered about town in helpless misery. But soon he was recognized. "Francesco, the idiot, the idiot!" was the cry that followed him up and down the streets. In those days those pitiable wretches were not regarded as sick people, but were made the defenseless butts of derision and were harried almost like wild beasts. Young and old ran after Francis, threw stones and filth at him, struck him and spit on him, tore at his clothes and his hair, and jostled him with cries of mockery. Far from being angry or resentful, Francis thanked God for this treatment, considering himself blessed for being humiliated for Christ's sake in the very streets where only a short while ago he had proudly accepted praise and homage. However, it was just this unbelievable humility and meekness on his part which incited the mob to gorge itself all the more on his apparent madness. The crowd grew larger and larger, and their mocking cries sounded in his ears like the yapping of a pack of dogs.

When they arrived at the Piazza del Comune and turned the corner of Santa Maria Maggiore the clamor penetrated into the shop of Bernardone. The old man hurried into the open and plainly heard the name of his Francesco being cried out by the mob. Overcome with grief and shame, he lost almost all control of himself. Rushing into the mob, he threw himself upon Francis like a wolf upon a lamb, as the early biographers state, dragged him into the house, and locked him in a dark chamber.

After keeping Francis on a scanty fare for several days, he thought the moment had come to move him to submission. At first he had recourse to words, pleading, and threatening; then he resorted to blows and finally to manacles. All to no avail. Francis remained unshakable. Moved by filial love he spoke kindly and gently to his father and tried to calm him. But Bernardone was implacable and demanded that he desist from his present mad conduct and return to the shop. Finally, having exhausted all means of persuasion, he again locked up the stubborn Francis and in sheer frustration hurried off on a business journey.*

In the meantime Donna Pica remained at home alone with Francis and his younger brother, Angelo. She was happy that Bernardone had left, for she naturally suffered greatly on account of the dissension between father and son. It was out of the question for her to remonstrate with Bernardone or to oppose him openly. Being a sensible and prudent woman she knew that anything of this sort would heighten his anger and worsen the position of Francis. She could only suffer in silence and place her trust in the Lord who, she was sure, would grant counsel and help at the right time. This time now seemed to have arrived. She resolved to avail herself of the occasion of her husband's absence to speak to Francis with the purpose of composing their dissension and by reconciling them restore peace and harmony to the family. With all the tenderness of which a harassed wife and mother was capable she argued with Francis, begged him, and pleaded with him, urging him to give up his eccentric manner of life.

But Francis was adamant. The pangs of his mother were, indeed, a sore trial to him, more so than his father's anger; but he could not think of yielding. He could and would belong to God alone. Of this Donna Pica herself finally became convinced. And because she was a good Christian woman she knew that one must obey God rather than men, and that not even parents have the right to oppose the recognized vocation of a child. She no longer pleaded with him. She unbound the fetters which shackled him, opened the door of

---

* Cel., I, 10–12; Socii, 16–18. According to the statutes of medieval municipalities a father was legally empowered to put a wasteful son behind bars. He was allowed to confine him to his own home, hold him a prisoner, and mistreat him at will; but he had to supply him with the necessary food. Cf. Pasquale Villari, *I primi due secoli della storia di Firenze* (Florence, 1893), vol. II, 47 *sq.*

his prison, and set him free. It was a step which only a mother's love and the fear of God could dare to take, one which boded great trouble for her.

Francis thanked his mother for freeing him and returned without delay to St. Damian, his refuge and the arena of his spiritual battles. He felt himself strong and determined as never before. He had passed the test as a candidate for knighthood with flying colors. Happy in his victory over himself and over the formidable obstacles which had confronted him, he faced the future with confidence. This calm confidence showed itself from this day forward in all his actions.[1] "As a true knight of Christ," writes Thomas of Celano, "he lent a deaf ear to all persecutions, and, unbroken and untouched by the wrongs done him, he thanked God for everything."[2] Even the efforts of the prince of darkness were in vain; nothing could make Francis turn from his purpose. "The brave knight of Christ," thus write the Three Companions, "laughed at his threats and begged the Lord that He might guide his steps."[3]

Meanwhile Bernardone had returned from his journey. His first act was to inquire about Francis. When he heard of his liberation and flight, he overwhelmed Pica with reproaches, and shouting threats and imprecations he stormed through the streets to St. Damian's, firmly determined to drag his son back as a prisoner or to banish him forever from his home. He could no longer endure the public dishonor brought upon him by his son. But there was a rude shock and sudden surprise in store for him when Francis approached him quietly and declared firmly that he was determined to serve God alone and that he was willing to suffer anything for the name of Christ. Bernardone realized that he could do nothing in the face of such determination. His rage turned into stony hardness of heart. Well and good, then his son was lost to him forever! No matter, as long as his own financial interests did not suffer. Brusquely he demanded the proceeds of the horse and goods.

Francis hastened to retrieve the money, for the pouch still lay in the window niche of the church. The glitter of gold softened the anger of Bernardone somewhat, yet his greed was not satisfied. Was that all? Did Francis have any intention of making later demands for his paternal inheritance? Was he determined to continue heaping dishonor and infamy upon his family by his eccentric and fanatic conduct? He was bound to make restitution in public for everything, to renounce every claim on his father's goods and property, and to be banished from his native country, just as the municipal statutes ordained for such cases.[4]

Bernardone's next step was to present his claims and demands to the civil authorities, who sent a court servant to St. Damian's with a summons for Francis. But the latter declined to heed the summons. He was polite, yet firm. He had dedicated himself to the sanctuary and was therefore no longer subject to civil courts.*

The city fathers themselves were relieved and happy when they discovered that they would not be burdened with the embarrassing affair. They recognized the claim of Francis and told the complainant: "Since your son has entered the service of God, he has been withdrawn from our jurisdiction. Only the Bishop is competent in this case."[5]

As a result Bernardone hurried to the episcopal residence and presented his complaint to the Church authorities. Bishop Guido, a man of discerning mind and prudent judgment, readily grasped the complexities of the situation. He had been taken into the confidence of Francis many times, and knew the young man well. He now summoned him in due form to answer his father's complaints. This time Francis answered the summons gladly: "I am ready to present myself before the Bishop, for he is the father and lord of souls."

Without further delay he appeared in front of the episcopal palace, where public receptions and other official transactions usually took place.[6] A curious throng had already gathered, tensely awaiting the outcome of this peculiar case over which all Assisi had been holding its breath. The Bishop turned to Francis with the words: "Your father is highly incensed against you and enraged. Return to him therefore the money which you hold, if you wish to be a servant of

---

* Francis was, in fact, no longer subject to secular courts on two counts: one, because he lived at St. Damian's, a church belonging to the bishop; and second, because he had dedicated himself to the service of this church as an oblate. For the relevant statutes see Fortini, 163, n. 9.

God. It may be ill-gotten money, and God does not wish that you use anything for the benefit of the Church, if its return will soothe his anger. Trust in God, my son, act bravely and fear not, for God Himself will be your helper and will provide in abundance. whatever is needed for the rebuilding of His Church."

These words naturally filled Francis with inexpressible joy and confidence. Quickly he placed himself between his father and the Bishop and cried out: "My Lord Bishop, I will return not only the money which is his with a joyful heart, but also the clothes which I wear on my body!" With these words he quickly took off the rich garments and gave them to his father. It could then be seen that the servant of God wore a hairshirt under his clothing, and swept away by an overpowering enthusiasm he also removed this in the presence of all. Then he said to his father Bernardone: "Until this hour I have called you my father on earth; henceforth I can say trustfully: My Father, who art in heaven! In His hands I have laid up all my treasures, in Him I have placed all my trust. From this hour I will serve the Lord."

The Bishop was unable to conceal his admiration and joy. He took Francis into his arms and covered him with his mantle. Many of those present were moved to tears. Only Bernardone, beside himself with rage and grief, snatched up the clothes and the money pouch and hurried away. A cry of horror and indignation swept through the throng when it was seen that he had not left enough of the clothing for Francis to cover his nakedness.[7]

This memorable event took place in the early spring of the year 1207.[8] Francis was then in his twenty-fifth year.

That was his final renunciation of all earthly things, his mystical espousals with his bride, Lady Poverty. It was she whom he had chosen according to the example of the crucified Lord and Saviour, she whom he had so ardently loved and yearned for and whom he had won, so to say, with his own blood in that valiant knightly combat with himself and the world. Never has all this been more beautifully described than in the immortal verses of Dante:

A dame, to whom none openeth pleasure's gate
More than to death, was, 'gainst his father's will,
His stripling choice: and he did make her his
Before the spiritual court, by nuptial bonds
And in his father's sight: from day to day
Then loved her more devoutly. She, bereaved
Of her first husband, slighted and obscure,
Thousand and hundred years and more, remain'd
Without a single suitor, till he came.[9]

PART TWO

THE PROVING OF
THE KNIGHT-ERRANT OF CHRIST

CHAPTER SEVEN

Francis Labors as Bondman of Christ

BERNARDONE had disappeared. The crowd dispersed. Bishop Guido continued to hold his mantle around Francis until his servants had found a garment to cover the half-naked man. They finally brought a well-worn garb of a peasant who was in the service of the Bishop. Francis, now a voluntary pauper, accepted the garment thankfully, marked a cross upon it with a piece of chalk which he happened to find there, and put it on. By doing so he plainly indicated, as St. Bonaventure states, that he was now in the knightly service of the Crucified, a genuine knight of the cross, a Crusader.[1] For it had always been the custom of the Crusaders to place the sign of the redemption on their clothing before setting out for the Holy Land.* Thus Francis also recognized himself and marked himself as a spiritual Crusader, and with a song in his heart he set out on his journey.

But whither? He was forcibly drawn to that labor service to which he was bound in fealty as a vassal of the Lord. The mandate of the Crucified of San Damiano was definite and urgent: "Francis, do you not see that My house is falling into ruins? Go and repair it!" These words burned like fire in his heart. He could have no rest until he had carried out his promise: "Gladly will I do so!"

---

* To this day the medieval formula of the blessing and imposing of the cross is found in the *Roman Pontifical*. (The Blessing and Imposing of the Cross for Those going forth to the Aid and Defense of the Christian Faith or for the Recovery of the Holy Land. *Benedictio et impositio Crucis proficiscentibus in subsidium et defensionem fidei Christianae seu recuperationem terrae sanctae*.) The solemn ceremony was conducted by the bishop from whose hands the Crusaders received the cross.

But for the present he could not return to St. Damian's. He had to wait until the storm had subsided. Furthermore, he could not see his way clear to rebuild the church, stripped as he was of all and poor as a beggar. But this fact did not cast even a shadow upon the calm surface of his soul, much less disturb it in its depths. Divine Providence had guided him so faithfully until now. Almost visibly and palpably and with gracious love it had stood at every crossroad to which his path had led. He was as "secure and free," as St. Bonaventure writes, as no other knight had been before him.[2] Thus he strode onward carefree and joyous at the side of his Lady Poverty. "Only the wall of the mortal body separated him from the beatific vision of the Most High," writes his oldest biographer.[3]

He was actually drunk with happiness. To display this happiness before the people, or even to let them surmise it, seemed like a desecration to him. He wanted to taste it to the full and let his heart sing out its rapture in silent solitude with God. His steps took wings. He rushed through the city gate on which was inscribed: *"Haec est via qua vaditur in Marchiam,"* and on which the words can be read today: "Through this gate the road leads to the March." He then took a northerly direction on one of the many footpaths which climb the ridge of Mount Subasio.

All nature seemed to be attuned to the song in his heart. It was just waking from its winter sleep. The air was pure, exhilarating, fragrant. Only on the heights and in the defiles of the hills was snow to be found. The hilly slopes drew fresh breath in the warm spring sun. The almond trees were in bloom. Young life broke forth from every pore of the earth. In the woods, the twitter of nesting birds. Everywhere else there brooded a solemn silence, as if the world were bowing in reverence to its Creator passing by.

A deep sense of devotion stirred Francis to his innermost being. The thought of God's greatness and goodness overwhelmed him. Under the stress of his emotion the songs of ancient chivalry rose to his lips and became hymns of praise to the Most High. A spiritual troubadour, he sang out the praises of God in the French tongue so clearly and loudly that field and forest rang with the sound.

He had already crossed the ridge of the hill and following the bank of the Chiagio he had passed Valfabbrica and was drawing near to Caprignone. The day was almost done. His loud singing had caught the attention of a group of bandits who infested the neighborhood. They broke in upon him, asking his name and his business in that part of the country. "What concern is that of yours?" he replied. "I am the herald of the great King." A royal messenger, indeed, in the ragged garment of a peasant! The man is half-witted, they thought. They took hold of him, rained blows upon him, tore off the shabby mantle he was wearing, and threw him into a ditch filled with snow. "Lie there, you loutish herald of God!" they cried out laughing, and then withdrew into the hills.[4]

Francis was overjoyed at this adventure, happy in the thought of suffering this mistreatment for the sake of the Lord. With great effort he worked his way out of the ditch, shook off the snow which clung to him, and, though shivering with cold, began to sing the praises of God more loudly than before.

It was dusk when he arrived at the Benedictine monastery of San Verecondo near Gubbio. He knocked at its door and humbly begged for shelter and for work to earn some decent clothes for himself.

The monks granted him lodging, gave him an old, torn workman's blouse, and assigned him to the kitchen to serve as a menial. All day long Francis performed the tasks of a drudge, his only food being some thin broth. Nobody made a move to supply him with better clothes. The evidently cultured young man, who now was obviously down at the heels and who despite meager food and hard labor always had a joyful though somewhat dreamy look, was a riddle to the monks. They regarded him as one of the many vagrants moving about the country, and they were really happy and relieved when he left. He took leave of them without the least sign of ill will over their treatment of him and directed his steps toward Gubbio.*

---

* The monks of San Verecondo were deeply chagrined when they later discovered what a holy guest it was they had treated so badly. They sent their prior to Francis, who had become a man of great renown in the meantime, to beg his forgiveness. The saint readily made friends with the monks and in later years

In Gubbio there lived an old friend and former comrade-in-arms, Count Frederico Spadalunga, who gave him a simple and poor garment, such as Francis had wished for.*

In this attire Francis set out on the return journey to San Damiano. However, he could not bring himself to pass by San Salvatore delle Pareti without visiting his friends, the lepers. What a joyous day for the poor, wretched creatures! This time he came indeed with empty hands and as a humble beggar; but now he was immeasurably closer to them, and his love for them was far more touching. Formerly he had made occasional visits, but now he made his home with them, shared their sufferings, privations, and sorrows, their joys, their food, and their hard pallets, and rendered to them every possible service. He washed their feet, bound up their sores, removed the foul matter from their wounds, cleansed and dried the festering swellings, and kissed them tenderly.[5] Far from experiencing his former loathing, this ministering to the lepers became for him sweetest joy. He himself bears witness to this in his Testament: "Whilst I was in sin, it seemed to me too bitter a thing to see lepers, but the Lord Himself led me amongst them, and I showed compassion to them. And when I left them what before had seemed bitter was changed into sweetness of soul and body."[6]

It was with great reluctance that he left his leper friends; but the mandate of the Crucified was urgent: "Go, and restore My house!" He took leave of the lepers with tears in his eyes, but promised that he would return and would remain their friend and protector all his life. Then he hurried to St. Damian.

It was a golden May day. The sun was shining and burning as brightly and as strongly in the heart of Francis as it was on the Umbrian plain. Don Pietro was again sitting before the chapel on a stone bench. With a critical and curious eye he surveyed the young

---

often visited them. Cf. Cel., I, 16; see also Faloci–Pulignani, *S. Francesco e il Monastero di San Verecondo presso Gubbio,* in: *Miscellanea francesc.,* X, (1906), 3–8.

* Cel., I, 16. That this friend and benefactor of Gubbio was Frederico Spadalunga can hardly be doubted considering the proofs proffered by Giuseppe Mazzatinti, *Miscellanea francescana,* V (1890), 76–78, and by Golubowich, O.F.M., *Archiv. francisc. hist.,* I (1908), 144–147.

pilgrim approaching the sanctuary, singing with so much abandon. Really, it was the former cavalier Francesco! Their meeting was exceedingly cordial. But Pietro had strong misgivings about remodeling the little church. Would not the renewed opposition of Bernardone have to be feared? And even if not, how could the costs be met, since both he and his guest were without means?

Francis simply quoted the words of Bishop Guido: "Trust in God, my son, act bravely and fear not, for God Himself will be your helper and will provide in abundance all that is needful for the building of His church." This satisfied the good priest. However, he wished that his companion would put on a religious garb and thus appear as a servant of the sanctuary. Francis hesitated for a moment, for he was neither a cleric nor a monk. Then he remembered that in the romances of chivalry one often met the hermit, "the holy man, who suffered for God." This decided him. He prepared a hermit's clothing for himself: a long garment like a habit, a leather girdle, shoes, and a staff. These he wore for two years until he received the miraculous calling to a higher state at Portiuncula.[7] He did not follow any particular religious Rule, but lived the life of the hermits as described in the epics of chivalry.*

Together with Lady Poverty he solved the problem of obtaining the necessary material for rebuilding the little church of St. Damian. He would follow the custom of the troubadours and minstrels and collect alms by singing in the streets and lanes of the city. With a quick decision he arose and went into Assisi. There he began to sing the praises of God, as if drunk in the spirit, using the French idiom of the poets of chivalry. As soon as the sound of his song had died, he began to plead for help for his little church, saying: "He who gives one stone will receive a single reward; who gives two stones, a twofold reward; but he who gives three stones, will receive a corresponding reward." Thus he went from house to house, repeating his song of praise and his plea for help, until he had reached every part of the city.

---

* "He followed no rule but that of his heart; no other discipline than that of a hermit in a romance of chivalry. (*Il ne suit nulle règle que celle de son coeur; point d'autre discipline que celle d'un solitaire dans un roman de chevalerie.*)" Gillet, *loc. cit.,* p. 758.

Many laughed at him and thought he had lost his mind; but others were moved to tears when they saw how quickly he had passed from his former frivolous and worldly life to such a close and ecstatic union with God. He felt no anger or resentment over laughter and mockery; on the contrary, he thanked God for it sincerely and ardently.

He soon had collected enough material to start his project. Several devoted friends came to give him a hand in his work. But a great many more came out of curiosity, gaping openmouthed at the rich merchant's son performing the rough labor of a mason. Francis invited all to help in the work, explaining to them in French how pleasing to God this project was, how much good had been done during the centuries in the little church which now was so in need of rebuilding, and what great blessings and graces the holy crucifix of St. Damian's would confer on all its devout clients. His example was even more effective than his words. He who had lived such a pampered life in the house of Bernardone, now carried stones and mortar on his shoulders and spent his bodily strength in labor such as chivalry demanded of the knight serving his supreme Lord. At the same time he was always in good cheer, and jested and sang gaily from morning till night. In this, too, he showed himself a follower of the champions of knighthood and proved true to the ideals of the epics of chivalry which in him, "the liege man of holy Christ," had become a reality.

Don Pietro observed his companion with admiration, but also some anxiety. He was aware of the luxurious life which Francis once lived in the world. Now he saw him laboring far beyond his strength, hardly granting himself the necessary food and rest. In the kindness of his heart and despite his own poverty Don Pietro therefore provided Francis with a particularly nourishing fare. At first Francis accepted Don Pietro's thoughtfulness with a thankful heart. But soon he began to feel a sense of shame in the belief that he had become unfaithful to his noble Lady Poverty. He said to himself: "Will you perhaps find a priest wherever you go who will show you such great kindness? The life you have now chosen is not the life of a poor man. Like the poor who go from door to door with a dish in their hands in which to put the remnants of food given them, you, too, must live from the offerings of charity — out of love for Him who was born poor, who lived as the poorest in this world, who hung as Victim poor and naked on the cross, and who was buried in a stranger's tomb."

He therefore took a bowl, went into the city, and started begging from door to door. While he was gathering all sorts of food in his bowl, the pampered merchant's son in him once more rose in rebellion. He could look back on a youth passed in luxury, and he had been accustomed to delicacies and dainty food. According to his own confession made later on he had never eaten anything which did not suit his taste! And now this change! A shudder of loathing seized him at first when he thought of eating the mess of leftovers; he could hardly get himself to look at it, much less to eat it. But with the true heroism of a knight of Christ he soon conquered himself and began to eat; and now it seemed to him as if he had never tasted such sweet and savory food.

Now he felt truly happy and this happy mood seemed to strengthen his weak and emaciated body. He was sure that now he could bear everything which was hard and bitter. Again there welled up in his heart a deep sense of gratitude toward God who once more had changed the bitter into sweetness, and his weakness into strength. He asked Don Pietro not to prepare any food for him any longer, nor to have it prepared for him by others. His beloved Lady Poverty would provide amply for his needs. From this hour on he lived solely on the food which he begged from door to door.[8]

His begging caused great excitement in Assisi. The people had, indeed, become accustomed to see him begging for his church, but it was simply inconceivable that he would go from house to house begging for morsels of food and eat the unsavory mixture, seated on some convenient doorstep and all aglow with happiness. Some of his fellow citizens were filled with admiration at the sight; others, however, mocked him and jeered at him wherever he showed himself.

His conduct caused his father boundless grief. Francis had been the joy of his heart as a child, his pride as a young man, and in his maturer years all his hope for the honor and greatness of his house. And now he was tramping about the city like a common beggar, greedily devouring the scraps from other people's tables, the like of which he formerly would not have touched. Bernardone was so overcome by shame and a sense of injury that he could not contain himself and cursed his son whenever he encountered him.

This was unbearable for Francis. His tender heart bled every time his father's imprecations reached his ears. In order to offset them and in a way render them ineffectual he chose a poor outcast by the name of Albert to be his companion and take his father's place.[9] "Come with me," he said to him, "I will share with you the alms which are given me. But when you see my father cursing me and I say to you: Bless me, father — then you are to make the sign of the cross over me and bless me in his name." Whenever the simple companion thus blessed Francis, the latter would say to his unnatural father: "Do you see that God can give me a father who utters blessings against your curses?"[10]

His brothers shared the hardness of Bernardone against Francis. One winter morning he was met by his brother, Angelo, in one of the churches.[11] Francis was half frozen, since he had been praying in the cold church for a long time, clothed as he was only in his thin hermit's garb. When passing him Angelo said jeeringly to a fellow citizen: "Tell Francis to sell you some of his sweat for a penny!" "I'm sorry," answered Francis in French, "I shall sell my sweat to the Lord for a much better price!"[12]

The rough work in rebuilding St. Damian's was almost finished when the above incident occurred. In addition to the work of reconstruction Francis also saw to the proper appointment of the interior of the sanctuary. Besides the lamp he had given on a former occasion, two other lights were to burn constantly before the figure of the Crucified. To supply these with oil Francis went into the city to beg.

It was while on this errand that his knightly heroism was put to a severe test. He happened to pass a house where he saw a group of young people gathered for song and dance. Everything was just as it had been in the days when he himself arranged these gay feasts, and he recognized a number of his former companions in the festive group. The contrast between then and now was too harsh and abrupt. Francis could not bring himself to beg in their presence, and quickly he turned away. But hardly had he taken a few steps when he became aware of his cowardice. He turned, walked to the gay group, and confessed before all that on their account he had been ashamed to beg. He then made the rounds smilingly and courageously, asking in French for alms to furnish oil for his church.[13]

At the end of 1207, or in the early spring of 1208, his work on the church of St. Damian was finished.[14] Again Francis knelt before the image of the Crucified and begged the Saviour to grant him light regarding his further course of action. It seemed to him that the command to restore the house of God referred also to the other churches in the vicinity. Close by there was another little church, dedicated to St. Peter, which was in the same dilapidated condition as St. Damian's had been.* He also restored this little church, for "in the sincere purity of his faith," as St. Bonaventure says, "he bore a special devotion to the Prince of the Apostles."[15]

Immediately after this, he undertook the restoration of the little church of the Virgin Mary, located in the plain below Assisi. Francis was often seen making his way from St. Damian's to this shrine. A legend said that it had been built in 352 by four hermits from Palestine. Its first name was "Mary of Josaphat," for allegedly it contained a relic from the grave of the Most Blessed Virgin in the valley of Josaphat, and was dedicated to the Assumption of Mary. In the sixth century it passed into the possession of the monks of Monte Cassino, and later on was called "Holy Mary of the Angels," because pious pilgrims declared they had heard the heavenly hosts singing in it the praises of God at various times. From the eleventh century on it belonged to the Benedictine monks of Monte Subasio. With it was a small piece of ground, from which the chapel derived its name of *Portiuncula,* or "small portion."[16] It now stood empty and deserted. With its cracked walls and bare interior it served the

---

* The church no doubt stood where now the Benedictine church of St. Peter stands today. This location was still outside the old city wall in the days of Francis.

shepherds and their flocks as a refuge against the inclemencies of the weather. When Francis saw its condition, sadness overcame him, and urged by his ardent love for heaven's Queen, he resolved to settle there and to rebuild the sanctuary.[17] That the Portiuncula would become the cradle of his own Order never entered his mind; indeed the foundation of an Order was at this time far from his thoughts.

Soon after the restoration of the shrine of Portiuncula God showed him that the mandate given him at St. Damian's did not concern only the material rebuilding of churches, but also the spiritual renovation of that world-wide Church which Christ had redeemed with His precious Blood.[18] Although he gave himself to this new task with greatest zeal as a loyal liege man of Christ, yet on occasion he returned to his first calling. In the year 1213, he rebuilt a church dedicated to the Blessed Virgin located between San Gemini and Porcaria.[19] Three years later he began the restoration of Santa Maria del Vescovado in Assisi. This church was so dilapidated that the roof covered only the part containing the Blessed Sacrament. In his ardent love for the eucharistic mystery Francis renovated the entire choir of the church and had a precious baldachin constructed over the main altar.[20]

The beauty and dignity of the churches was always close to his heart. In the first years of the Order he made the rounds in the villages near Assisi, carrying a broom with him in order to clean out the neglected sanctuaries. The first thing he did on these visits was to exhort the people to penance. Then he gathered the clergy in a separate place, urged them to be zealous in the care of souls, and adjured them particularly to keep churches, altars, and everything pertaining to the celebration of the sacred mysteries in a proper and clean condition.[21] Even in his *Testament* he had the deeply touching words written down: "The Lord gave me such faith in churches, that I would with simplicity thus adore and say: We adore Thee Most Holy Lord Jesus Christ, here, and in all the churches throughout the world, and we bless Thee, because by Thy Holy Cross Thou hast redeemed the world. Afterwards the Lord gave me, and gives me still, such faith in priests who live after the manner of the Holy Roman Church, on account of their Orders, that if they persecuted me I would still have recourse to them. And if I had the wisdom of Solomon, and found priests poor and ignorant according to the world, I would not preach in their parishes against their will. And these priests and all others I am resolved to hold in respect, love and honor as my lords: and I will not consider any sin in them, because I behold in them the Son of God, and they are my lords. I act thus because in this world I see nothing corporally of the Most High Son of God, but His Most Holy Body and Blood, which they consecrate and receive, and which they alone administer to others. And these Most Holy Mysteries I desire to venerate and honor above all things, and to preserve in precious tabernacles."[22]

To the liege man of "Holy Christ" all this meant service to be rendered by him as a loyal vassal, for the crucified Lord and Saviour had bidden him: "Francis, do you not see that My house is falling into ruin? Go and rebuild it!"*

---

* In his *Testament* Francis declares expressly that the Lord had given him this deep and lively faith in churches, its servants, and mysteries after his renunciation of the world, that is, after the revelation made to him by the Crucified at St. Damian. He says: "After that I tarried yet a little and forsook the world. And the Lord gave me such faith in churches . . . etc." *Test., Opusc.*, 78 *sq.*

CHAPTER EIGHT

The Herald of the Great King

EVER since the Crucified had spoken to him at St. Damian, Francis was aware that he was called to more than the material rebuilding of churches. Did not the ideals of chivalry demand that the knight labor and fight for the increase of the Christian faith, the extension of the kingdom of God on earth, and the defense of the Church of Christ? Thomas of Celano states with an air of certainty that the mandate of the Crucified at St. Damian was meant directly for the rebuilding of that Church "which Christ had bought with His own Blood," but that Francis undertook the physical reconstruction of churches at first out of humility, since he was "to pass step by step from the flesh to the spirit."*

The Saint did actually feel and also declare himself a "herald of the Great King." A *herald* was an official of knightly birth who delivered the invitations or challenges at feasts and tournaments, directed the preparation and the course of the contests, and had charge of the entire ceremonial of the court. But *herald* meant also, in medieval Latin, a preacher, the messenger of the faith, the proclaimer of divine truth.[1] Even before Francis was able to undertake the rebuilding of St. Damian he wandered through field and forest, filling them with the melody of his *chansons,* his hymns of praise to the "Great King." At the same time his

* "For though the divine message made to him was regarding that Church which Christ had bought with His own Blood, yet he did not wish to reach the heights at once, since he was to pass step by step from the flesh to the spirit." (*Nam licet de illa Ecclesia divinus ei factus sit sermo, quam Christus proprio sanguine acquisivit, noluit repente fieri summus, paulatim de carne transiturus ad spiritum.*)

burning zeal urged him more and more not only to sing the praises of God, but to preach the word of God itself.

The apostolate fitted perfectly into his conception of knighthood. It was nothing new to join the figure of a hero with that of an apostle. In the Heliand, a ninth-century epic written in the Old Saxon tongue, the theme is the life of the Saviour. Christ is called throughout "the Suzerain Liege Lord, the Prince of princes, the mightiest King, the Emperor of heaven," while the twelve Apostles appear as "the heroes, whom Christ the Ruler of all has chosen."[2] He is "the Liege Lord of the warriors." Peter is "the expert swordsman," "the high-spirited fighter in the presence of his Prince," "the bravest of warriors"; John is "the dearest of the fighters, the most beloved"; Thomas is "the faithful warrior, who desires to suffer with Christ, the Liege Lord, to stand by his Commander and to die with Him."[3] With the development of the Christian idea of chivalry, the Apostles, too, became knights in the service of their Master, of His word, and of His kingdom. Francis was deeply influenced, consciously or unconsciously, by this widespread conception. He was waiting only for word from above to pass over into the orbit of apostolic activity. This word was not long in coming.

About two years had passed since he had heard the momentous words: "Francis, do you not see that My house is falling into ruins? Make haste and rebuild it!" He was attending Mass one cold morning in the chapel of Portiuncula. It was the feast of St. Mathias, the twenty-fourth of February, 1209 (1208?). The priest read the gospel describing the sending of the Apostles to preach. Francis knew barely enough Latin to follow the reading. Immediately after Mass he asked the priest to explain more fully the pericope of the apostolic mission. When he was told that a true disciple of the Lord should not possess gold nor silver nor copper, neither scrip nor purse nor a staff, neither shoes nor two coats, but stripped of all earthly things should preach the kingdom of God and penance, he exclaimed jubilantly: "This is what I desire! This is what I seek! This is what my whole heart craves!"[4]

With one bright flash this ray from heaven lighted up his

future course of action. He was to be, as Brother Jordan of Jano remarks, "an imitator of evangelical poverty and at the same time a zealous preacher of the gospel";[5] he was to renounce the world completely and yet be active as an apostle in the world and for the world. Both together, apostolic poverty and preaching, apostolic world-renunciation and apostolic world-activity, were to be equally essential elements of the calling of the new knight-errant of Christ, just as they were essential to the calling of the Apostles, and just as they were inseparably united in the Gospel of the sending of the disciples.*

Without a moment's delay Francis put the words of the Gospel into practice, threw away staff and scrip and shoes, and put on a very simple garb. Then, as Celano writes, "he began to preach penance to all with great ardor and joy of the spirit, edifying his hearers by his simple speech and noble thoughts. His word was as a flaming fire, penetrating to the innermost core of their hearts and filling the minds of all with wonderment."[6]

The impression which the new apostle made was so powerful that not only did great numbers of people convert from evil ways,[7] but several high-minded men resolved to join the preacher and to make his life and work their own. The first recruits were Bernard of Quintavalle, who was of noble birth, and the priest Peter Catanii. Francis conducted them to the Church of St. Nicholas in Assisi and in their presence had the Gospel book opened in order to ascertain whether they, too, were called to the life of apostolic poverty and apostolic preaching. Three times the holy book was opened at random and each time their eyes fell on the story of the sending of the disciples. Then Francis turned to his first-born companions and said: "Brothers, this is our life and our Rule and of all those who would join our company. Go then, and do what you have heard."[8] They went, sold all their goods

---

* We restrict ourselves in the following exposition to the most necessary accounts of the preaching activity of St. Francis and his companions. A more detailed account can be found in the fifteenth and sixteenth chapters of our previous work: *The Ideals of St. Francis,* transl. by Berchmans Bittle, O.F.M.Cap. (New York: Benziger Bros., 1925).

and handed the proceeds to the poor; then they set out with Francis on their first mission journey.

It was a very unique manner, however, in which they did their preaching. The saintly leader strolled onward, as usual singing songs of chivalry in French in which he glorified and praised the Most High and His infinite goodness. Whenever he met people on the roads or in the streets of the villages and towns, he exhorted them to love and fear God and to do penance for their sins. Brother Giles, however, who in the meantime had become the fourth member of the brotherhood, admonished the people to listen to Francis and to believe him because his counsel was above reproach.[9]

After a short while four others joined the little band.[10] These also were reminded by the founder of their calling to apostolic activity with the words: "Let us consider well our vocation, most beloved brothers, and bear in mind that God in His mercy has called us unto the salvation not only of our souls but of many, that we go through the world exhorting all peoples by word and example to do penance for their sins and to observe the commandments of God. Fear not if you are looked upon as mean and contemptible and ignorant, but preach penance with courage and simplicity; trusting that the Lord, who has overcome the world, will speak in you and through you by His Spirit to move all to be converted to Him and to observe His commandments."[11]

After a short period of training to acquaint them with their new calling and its work, they were ready to set out on their tour of preaching. First of all Francis marked a cross on the ground, the arms pointing to the corners of the globe, and sent the brothers two and two into the four directions. Whenever they entered a town or village, a hamlet, or a house, they spoke the greeting of peace and urged everyone to love and fear the Creator of heaven and earth, and to keep His commandments. Toward everyone, friend or foe, they were gentle and kind, and their conduct as well as their words edified all and gained them for God. After a time they returned to their starting point at Portiuncula, sought recollection in prayer and contemplation, related their experiences, and fortified each other to new, unceasing labors in the Lord's vineyard.[12]

In the meantime they had grown to twelve, a full apostolic group. Francis now felt that the time had arrived to obtain the approval of the Church for their mode of life and a formal commission or mandate for their apostolate of preaching. "Brothers," he said, "I see that God deigns to increase our brotherhood. Let us then go to our Mother, the holy Roman Church, and tell the Pope what the Lord has begun to do through us, that we may continue what we have begun according to His will and command."[13]

Their pilgrimage to Rome became another missionary journey, similar to those that had preceded. In the Eternal City they found an unexpected and powerful friend in Cardinal John Colonna. This Cardinal saw in the unpretentious poor man of Assisi the future champion of God's cause and introduced him to the papal court with the words: "I have found a most perfect man, who desires to live after the manner of the gospel and to observe evangelical perfection; through him, as I believe, God intends to renew the Church in the whole world."[14]

Innocent III himself had seen in a vision a man who supported the church of the Lateran with his shoulders, and when Francis appeared before him he exclaimed: "Truly, this is the man who will support the Church of Christ by word and deed."[15] Having tested the constancy of the twelve friars, he approved their Rule and their apostolate with the words: "Go then, brothers, with the blessing of God, and preach penance to all as God will deign to inspire you. And as soon as the Almighty has blessed you in numbers and in grace, report to Us, and We shall concede to you even greater things and commit even greater tasks to you with full confidence."* The Pope added expressly that all the disciples of Francis should be entitled to exercise the apostolate in the

---

* Socii, 49; cf. Cel., II, 17. The words "greater things and greater tasks" indicate that the friars would soon be allowed to preach dogmatic or scriptural sermons, while for the present they were restricted to preaching penance or to moral sermons. Cf. Felder, *The Ideals of St. Francis* (New York: Benziger Bros., 1925), pp. 341–343.

entire world as long as they received the permission to preach from their founder.[16] He then admitted the twelve friars to the tonsure, receiving them into the ranks of the clergy, who alone were entitled to exercise the office of preaching.[17]

Herein lay the decisive and far-reaching importance of the papal mission. Until then the men of Assisi had spoken to the people only brief though stirring exhortations to do penance and to amend their lives, as the Three Companions expressly state.[18] It had been a purely lay apostolate, such as could be exercised without formal authorization on the part of the Church. "From now on, however," the same biographers continue, "blessed Francis exercised the office of preaching in the fuller and wider sense; for he was now a preacher strengthened by apostolic authority."[19] This is in agreement with the description which the Three Companions give of his apostolic activity.[20] Thomas of Celano is also in full accord when he pens the following inimitable description of the preaching of Francis and its results:

"The most brave knight of Christ, Francis, traversed the cities and hamlets announcing the kingdom of God, not in the persuasive words of human wisdom, but in the word and power of the Holy Spirit, preaching peace, teaching salvation, and penance unto the remission of sins. Sustained by the apostolic authority granted him he bore himself in all things with perfect confidence, without flattery and vain eloquence. He understood not how to palliate the faults of certain of his hearers, but attacked them fearlessly; far from defending the life of sinners, he impugned it with keen reproof. Since he had proved by his own actions what he required of others, and therefore feared no rebuke, he preached the truth with such courage that even the most learned men, however great their fame and dignity, admired his words and were seized with wholesome fear at his appearance. The men pressed about him, the women flocked to him, the clerics hastened to him, even the religious eagerly sought to see and hear the man of God, who appeared to them as a man from another world. Every age and sex hastened to behold the wonders which God worked through His servant in the world.

"Everyone, whether he met Francis in person or knew him only from report, was convinced that a new light from Heaven had been sent to the earth, to dispel the night of darkness which had sunk upon almost the entire world, so that no one found a remedy. For such an abysmal godlessness and such a deadening indifference had overcome almost all men, that they could scarcely be awakened from the death of their old and deeply rooted vices. Then Francis alone shone forth like a glittering star in the darkest night, and spread as a radiant dawn over the darkness. Thus it came to pass that soon the face of the earth was renewed and showed a joyous mien, without even a trace of its former ugliness. Gone was the long drought, and on the swaying field the grain ripened unto the harvest. The hitherto unpruned vine put forth its sprouts full of heavenly aroma, unfolded of its own strength sweet-smelling blossoms, and matured into the fruit of honesty and virtue. Everywhere prayer and praise resounded, so that many, because of the life and teaching of most blessed Father Francis, renounced the care of earthly things, came to the knowledge of themselves and aspired only after the love and the reverence of the Creator.

"Many of the people, nobles and citizens, clerics and laics, moved by divine inspiration, began to join the holy Francis, and desired to serve as knights under his direction and leadership. All these the Holy Spirit, as a stream overflowing with heavenly grace, bedewed with His choicest gifts and adorned the soil of their hearts with the flowers of virtue; for he was the chosen work-master, by whose example, rule and doctrine, and under whose standard, which he carried aloft, the Church is renewed, and the threefold body of knights leads the triumphal march of the elect. But to all others likewise he marked the course of life and pointed out to men and women of every station the way of salvation."[21]

At first only Umbria and central Italy experienced these blessings of the Franciscan apostolate. The Franciscan preachers ventured into the more distant regions only by way of exception and only for a time. In a short while, however, the number of friars increased so greatly that they could be sent into all the provinces of Italy.[22] In 1216, Bishop James of Vitry wrote that the new apostles had conquered the whole of Italy from Lombardy to Apulia and Sicily and had spread the greatest blessings everywhere.[23] At the Pentecost Chapter of 1217, a concentric march into the northern countries was begun. In 1219 the "brothers of penance of Assisi" invaded France; in 1221, Germany; and England in 1224.[24]

Already in the lifetime of their founder the disciples of Francis were active throughout the West. The prediction of Cardinal John of St. Paul that Francis would renew the Church in the whole world was fulfilled in a striking manner. Thomas of Celano could declare as an eyewitness: "At a time when the doctrine of the gospel was everywhere neglected, Francis was sent by God to give testimony unto the truth in the whole world after the manner of the apostles. . . . While still living among us sinners he wandered and preached throughout the whole world."[25]

Though this was true in general only of the Christian Occident, Francis was determined to bring the Gospel also to the Mohammedans in the East, the West, and the South.[26] His brotherhood had been founded only three years (1212) when he undertook the mission. Thomas of Celano writes of it: "Glowing with divine love and burning with the desire for martyrdom, the Blessed Father Francis set out for the regions of Syria, in order to preach the Christian faith and penance."[27] But the ship had not yet left the Adriatic Sea when a violent storm cast it on the Dalmatian coast. Since the season was well advanced it was impossible to undertake another journey to the Orient. Francis therefore had to return to Italy with his companions by way of Ancona.[28]

Since there was no prospect for the time being of coming to grips with Oriental Islamism, he shortly after (1213-1215) journeyed on foot through Lombardy and southern France to the Spanish-Moroccan kingdom of the Saracens. King Alfonso VIII, with the aid of the pope and the Spanish Orders of Knights, had just achieved the smashing victory of Navas de Tolosa over the Moors (June 16, 1212). Francis was anxious to grasp this opportunity to preach the Gospel to the defeated Sultan Mohammed-el-Naser and his adherents and to gain the crown of martyrdom for himself.* His desire for this crown was so strong and his yearning of such driving force that he at times outran his companion, Brother Bernard of Quintavalle, as if carried away by a spiritual intoxication. But this time, too, it was not granted him to reach the goal he so ardently longed for. Hardly had he set foot on the Pyrenean Peninsula when God sent a severe illness which forced him to retrace his steps without gaining his objective.[29]

But he did not allow himself to become discouraged. Some time later, after he had dispatched brothers into the most distant regions of Europe (1219), he set out with his "guardian," Peter Catanii, for Damietta in Egypt, where the armies of the Crusaders were engaged in a bitter struggle with the legions of Sultan Melek-el-Khamil.[30] "It should not appear," writes Jordan of Giano, "as if the blessed Father sought repose while he sent forth the brothers to suffer and to labor for Christ; on the contrary, in the valorous chivalry of his soul he wished to precede all on the way of Christ. While he was thus sending forth his sons to the perilous preaching of the faith, he himself, burning with love for the passion of Christ, braved the dangers of a sea journey, reached the infidels, and hastened to the Sultan."[31] It was indeed a hazardous undertaking since the Sultan had placed a price on the head of every Christian![32] Francis, however, bore himself with such gentleness and humility, and at the same time with such courage and holy daring that the Sultan did him no harm, but even listened willingly to his words, kept him as his guest for about a week, and allowed him to preach the Christian faith. But as soon as he learned that Francis attacked the errors of Islam, he had him escorted back to the camp of the Christians under military guard. Once more the Saint had failed to reach the greatly coveted goal — the conversion of the enemies of Christ and death as a martyr for Christ.

---

* Thomas of Celano gives the name of the Sultan as Miramamolin, which means Miralmoslemin, that is Amir al Moslemin or Prince of the Moslems, the official title of the sultan of Morocco. The personal name of the sultan whom Francis wished to convert was Mohammed-el-Naser.

Other friars were more fortunate. Brothers Berard, Peter, Otto, Adiutus, and Accursius were sent by Francis to the Moors, and they preached first in the Saracen city of Seville. After being subjected to tortures in that city, they were deported to Morocco and finally, after suffering other gruesome tortures, were beheaded by the Sultan in person (January 1, 1220). The joy of Francis over their martyrdom was as great as if he himself had shared their glory. When he received the news of their death he exclaimed jubilantly that God had given him five genuine Friars Minor. And turning toward Portugal, he blessed the city of Alenquer, whence the martyrs had set out.[33]

He then put his hand to the final revision of the older Rule (1221). In this Rule there are two chapters on the apostolate, of which the one (XVII) treats of preaching among the faithful, and the other (XVI) of the mission among "the Saracens and other infidels."[34] Two years later he wrote the final Rule, in which these two chapters are embodied in a shorter form, but with essentially the same contents.[35] Regarding the going of missioners to the infidels Francis gives these definite directions: "Should any friar, moved by divine inspiration, desire to go among the Saracens or other infidels, he shall ask leave to go from his Minister Provincial. But the Ministers shall not grant leave except to those whom they deem fit to be sent" (XII).

In these words missionary work among the Moslems and other unbelievers is proclaimed an essential part of the activity of the Order of Friars Minor; the Saint even regarded it as the noblest task of the Order. Whenever he spoke of the labors undertaken by the friars in obedience, he said: "The most sublime obedience, in which flesh and blood have no part, consists in this that one should go, inspired by God, among the infidels, both in order to save one's fellowman and from a desire for the death of martyrdom. To ask this obedience of the superiors, is specially pleasing to God."[36]

No religious founder, no religious institute before Francis, had spoken such language. Great as was the number of missionaries who had gone forth into the world, the Poverello was the first to incorporate in a Rule the apostolate among unbelievers. In fact, he was the first Occidental to bring the faith to countries outside of Europe. Since the days of the Apostles he was the first preacher of the Gospel who emblazoned on his banner the conversion of the whole world.

How did the merchant's son come to this sublime, far-reaching concept? He knew, of course, that he was called to the apostolate of preaching, because the Gospel of the sending of the Apostles had been for him a direct revelation. But who showed him the way to the "Saracens and other infidels"? How explain the fact that he followed in the footsteps of the Crusader knights to the East, the South, and the West, and regarded a martyr's death for the faith as the supreme achievement? Simply by the fact that he was most deeply imbued with the knightly ideal of the era of the Crusades. In the main the purpose of crusading knighthood was to do battle against the Saracens. Whatever was not Christian was Saracenic in the eyes of Christendom at that time.[37]

Every true knight took the cross and journeyed over the seas. "Only knights without God, without good, without honor and valor, pure cowards and poltroons remain at home," were the words of a Crusader song.[38] And again: "Here in this world the knights may not live free of cares. They must defend the Christian faith and shed their blood for the faith."[39] Happy the one who merited to die in battle waged against the infidels! He was regarded as a martyr for Christ and the faith and entered paradise like Roland, Oliver, Turpin, and the rest of Charlemagne's paladins:

> Nor fire feared they nor the sword.
> In truth 'twas granted by the Lord
> What they desired with ardent glow,
> The while they lived on earth below:
> Achieved the martyr's bright renown
> And heaven's everlasting crown.[40]

This is fully in accord with the declarations made by Francis regarding the missions among "the Saracens and other infidels." It would be a waste of time to try to prove that he was inspired by the ideals of the Crusades and that he undertook and recommended the apostolate among the unbelievers precisely because he was truly and wholly a knight of Christ.

Yet Christ's knight-errant of Assisi understood this apostolate in an essentially different sense than the Crusaders. Their entire aim, their effort, and all their fighting was an apostolate of the sword. Just as missionizing in the Middle Ages had been often, only too often, done with the sword, so also the Crusaders aimed at conquering Islam chiefly with military and political means and rendering it subject to Christendom. That the archenemy of the Christian faith could be checked in the East as well as in the West only by force of arms is evident; however, not seldom efforts were made to impose the Christian faith on the conquered by the sword. Characteristic in this regard is the *Song of Roland,* the noblest and most important of the hero epics, which in Francis' day was very popular and had given mighty inspiration to Francis himself. As is well known, it praises Charlemagne and his paladins as the conquerors of the Saracens in Spain. After the decisive victory of Saragossa it proclaims jubilantly that death or baptism awaited the vanquished: "The King believes in God, he desires to perform his service, and the Bishops bless the waters. The infidels are led to the baptismal font. If even one resists Charles, the King orders him to be hanged or burned or beheaded. Far more than one hundred thousand are baptized as true Christians, only not the empress (the wife of the Saracen emperor). She is to be led a captive to gentle France: the King wishes that she be converted from love."[41] Francis, however, spiritualized the idea of the Crusades. With his vision fixed on the example of the Apostles, he went forth to the Saracens as a preacher of the Gospel, of peace, of penance, of grace, and of true spiritual freedom.

Yet one thing the apostolate of Francis had in common with that of the Crusaders: the source of inspiration as well as the goal of both was knightly fealty in the service of their sovereign Liege Lord, Jesus Christ.

CHAPTER NINE

The Knight of Christ and His Liege Lord

FROM the moment when Francis became a liege man of the sovereign Lord, his devotion to Him knew no bounds. Whereas formerly his only endeavor had been to please the great ones of this world in order to reach the rank of nobility, his sole aim now was to know and to perform his task as liege man and knight of Christ. The mere thought of this sublime calling gave him the strength to make even the most heroic sacrifices.[1] All his life, as Thomas of Celano says, it was a matter of honor to him "to put his hands to deeds of valor."[2] According to his biographers he proved himself always, everywhere, and under all circumstances as "the most valiant knight of God," who "went into battle wearing the armor of Christ," as "the new champion of Christ," as "the indefatigable and invincible captain of the new militia of Christ."[3]

The new militia of Christ of which he was the captain was to be inspired by the same ideals. All his disciples, from the elegant nobleman down to the last and least of the little brothers, he considered and treated as true knights of the Saviour. One day near Rieti he met a young knight of the family of Tancredi, who, mounted on a proud charger and accoutered in shining armor, drew all eyes to himself. "Sir Knight," said Francis approaching him, "armor, sword and spurs are empty glamor. Would you not like to wear a coarse rope instead of the girdle, the cross of Christ instead of the sword, and the dust and dirt of the road instead of the spurs? Follow me. I shall make you a knight of

Christ."[4] That was the conversion of Brother Angelus Tancredi, and that was the conception which every candidate had to have of his calling in order to enter the new militia of Christ. When the simple, yet ingenious Brother Giles asked the Saint for the habit of the Order, Francis gave him to understand: "Most beloved, God has bestowed on you a great gift. If the emperor came to Assisi and wished to choose one of the townsmen as his knight or chamberlain, many, indeed, would desire to be chosen. How much more ought you to be glad that the Lord has chosen you from among all and called you to His own court."[5] This episode is very enlightening. The companions were to be not merely common knights, but proved, trusted, much beloved paladins of the Lord. In view of the eminent qualities of Brother Giles the Saint declared outright: "This is my Knight of the Round Table!"[6]

The twelve heroic champions of King Arthur were, indeed, in his eyes the models for his companions. When speaking of zealous and brave friars he was wont to cry out jubilantly: "These are the friars who are my Knights of the Round Table!"[7] On one occasion he reminded a novice of Charles the Great and his twelve paladins in their battle for Christ, the Church, and the faith, and he added: "Charles, the emperor, Roland, Oliver, and all the Paladins and valiant men, excelled in battle by their bravery, pursued the infidels in bitter struggle until they were destroyed, gained memorable victories over them and finally died as holy martyrs in the defense of the faith of Christ. But now, on the contrary, there are many who gain the applause of men and honor by merely relating their great deeds."[*] From this it is evident not only that

---

* *Spec. perf.*, c. 4. Blessed Brother Giles applied this directly to slothful fellow religious: "Many enter religion and do not those things which are becoming to religion; and such are like a peasant who puts on the arms of Roland and would not know how to fight with them; for all men do not know how to ride the horse Bayard [of Roland], nor when sitting on him do they know how to avoid a fall. I do not consider it a great thing to enter the court of a king, nor do I think it a great thing to receive gifts from a king, but I do esteem it a great thing to know how to conduct oneself in the royal court as it behooves. The court of the Great King is the religious state. . . . " *Dicta b. Aegidii Assis.*, Ad Claras Aquas (1905), 63. Cf. *The Golden Sayings of Blessed Brother Giles of Assisi*, transl. by Paschal Robinson, O.F.M. (Dolphin Press, 1907), p. 61 f.

Francis was acquainted with the *Song of Roland* and the Legend of King Arthur, but also that he saw in the paladins of the Frankish epic poem and of the Breton hero romances the types of his own knighthood of Christ and of the militia of Christ. The Lord had called him to be a knight-errant of Christ; he would prove himself a true paladin of Christ.

The full import which this conception had for Francis becomes clear when the feudal relation between the knight and his lord is considered. The liege man was bound to follow his lord into war, to fight at his side, and to stand by him unto death. This was regarded as knightly *fealty,* loyal vassalage. This naturally brought about a relationship between the liege man and his lord which was not merely servile but personal. This personal character was accentuated by the so-called *homage* which was owed by the vassal. In virtue of this homage the knight recognized the lord as his superior and master and vowed reverence and assistance, together with the affection of a loyal friend. Both, knightly fealty and knightly homage and service, were vowed by the liege man kneeling, placing his folded hands in the hands of his liege lord, and rendering the oath of vassalage. For the knight-errant of Assisi it was self-understood that he was irrevocably dedicated to his Lord in fealty and loving homage.

Faithful service in arms made the knight a *loyal man of honor* (*homo legalis*). This loyalty must never waver, just as God's fidelity never wavers:

> Be true — loyal without fail,
> As God Himself is ever true,
> And hateth the false knave, —

that was the injunction given to the knight.[8] To accuse him of disloyalty was the gravest insult one could offer a knight.[9] Felony, the violation of fealty, outlawed the knight, was punished by death, and led to the society of the "sulphur burning hordes" of devils.[10]

Francis was most deeply imbued with these concepts. He knew that he and his brothers were under a twofold obligation of loyal fealty to the "Lord of lords."[11] First, because the Saviour called upon all men to follow Him,[12] and because He condemned all disloyalty committed against Him,[13] and secondly, because He had chosen Francis and his companions to be His knights and trusted comrades. For this reason Francis constantly admonished his friars to walk at the side of the Saviour step by step, to emulate His example, and to live after the manner of His Gospel.

Already in the first Franciscan Rule were found the words: "The rule and life of these brothers is this: namely, to live in obedience, and chastity and without property, and to follow the doctrine and footsteps of our Lord Jesus Christ."[14] In the Rule of 1221, Francis again admonishes: "Let us therefore hold fast the words, the life and teaching and holy gospel of Him who deigned to pray His Father for us, and to manifest His name to us. . . . Let us therefore desire nothing else, wish for nothing else, and let nothing else please us, nor delight us except our Creator and Redeemer and Saviour."[15] From his deathbed he wrote his last will and testament for St. Clare and her daughters: "I, little brother Francis, wish to follow the life and poverty of our Most High Lord Jesus Christ and of His Most Holy Mother, and to persevere therein to the end. And I beseech you all, my ladies, and counsel you, that you may live always in this most holy life and poverty."[16]

Leading all the others, Francis was himself the most faithful follower of the Saviour. The following of Christ in all conditions of life, in thought and action, in commission and omission — practical, energetic, unswerving, and persevering following of Christ is the secret of the Assisian knight-errant. In great things and in small, in the hidden life of the soul as well as in the exterior conduct of life, he sought to become like Christ and to carry out His Gospel without the least mitigation, according to the letter as well as to the spirit. It is a somewhat naïve and extravagant yet on the whole faithful picture which Bartholomew of Pisa draws in the work: *On the Conformity of the Life of St. Francis with the Life of the Lord Jesus*. The basic thought of this work had been previously expressed in the first lines of the *Fioretti*: "Conformity of St. Francis with Christ. Let us consider in the first place that the glorious St. Francis was conformed to the Life of the blessed Christ in all the acts of his life."

This conviction is shared after all by the historians and biographers of Francis of every age. Already Thomas of Celano had written: "His supreme endeavor, his most ardent wish and highest aim was to observe the holy gospel in all things and above all things, and to follow perfectly, with all zeal, with the fullest ardor of his spirit, with all the love of his heart, the teachings of our Lord Jesus Christ, and to follow His example. In constant meditation he reflected on His words, and with deep intentness he pondered on His works. . . . In my opinion the sainted Francis was a most holy mirror of the holiness of our Lord and the image of His perfection."[17] The great genius and writer Goerres says of him: "If since the days of the apostles the Saviour has found one who has walked after Him in all His footsteps, followed His example in all His teachings, and clung to Him with all the strength of his soul, it was this inspired and exalted soul, who, sunning himself ceaselessly in His light, himself became a light-bearer, reflecting not only His splendor but His very image."[18]

The inviolable fealty of the knight-errant of Assisi reached its zenith in his complete self-dedication, his ardent yet tender *homage*. From the days of Spoleto and San Damiano his life was a song of pure love and praise, homage and adoration. The Three Companions relate: "From the time of his conversion until his death he loved Christ with his whole heart, having the memory of Him ever in mind, praising Him with his lips, and glorifying Him in good works. So ardently and so tenderly did he love the divine Saviour that on hearing His sweet Name he became enraptured and cried out: 'Heaven and earth should bow before the Name of the Lord!' "[19] He wrote to the friars of the General Chapter: "When you hear His Name, adore ye with fear and reverence, prostrate on the ground; the Lord Jesus Christ, such is the Name of the Most High Son of God."[20]

In deeply touching words "the brothers who lived with him would delight in telling how he daily and constantly occupied himself with Jesus when conversing, how sweet and charming was his discourse, how gentle and loving his talk of Jesus," declares Thomas of Celano, and he adds: "His tongue spoke out of the fullness of his heart, and

the stream of enraptured love which filled his soul overflowed outwardly. Always was he occupied with Jesus. Jesus he bore in his
heart, Jesus in his mouth, Jesus in his eyes, Jesus in his ears, Jesus
in his hands, Jesus in all his members. Oh, how often he forgot
earthly food at table when hearing the Name of Jesus, or pronouncing it, or thinking of it; seeing, he then saw not; and hearing, he
heard not. Often, too, when thinking of Jesus on his journeys, or
singing of Him, he lost sight of his way and cried out to all elements
inviting them to praise Jesus."[21] The mere sight of a church or of a
cross, a single word about the Saviour or His blessed Mother sufficed
to immerse him in profound contemplation.* With great urgency he
constantly besought the Lord in his prayers to grant him the grace
of perfect love: "I beseech Thee, O Lord, that the fiery and sweet
strength of Thy love may absorb my soul from all things that are
under heaven, that I may die for love of Thy love, as Thou didst
deign to die for love of my love."[22] All his prayers to Christ ended
in the one refrain "to be dissolved and be with Christ," as Celano
says.[23] The same biographer states that his devotion to Christ was
anchored in the unbroken contemplation of His life, especially of
His Incarnation and sacred Passion.[24] His devotion to the latter
deserves a more detailed treatment, for it is only the *mystery of the
cross* which reveals to us the full meaning and the full scope of the
Saint's knightly fealty and knightly homage to Christ.

He had been knighted by the Crucified and for this reason he
was conscious of a heavy debt of gratitude toward the suffering
Saviour. And not only a debt of gratitude, but a debt of service as
well. Christian knighthood and the example of the Crusaders and
of the religious knights of his time, all dedicated to the liberation
of the land where the Saviour suffered and died, gave further
impetus to his love and devotion to the Crucified.

When a squire was raised to the rank of knighthood he first
promised, in the course of the religious ceremony, "to attend Mass

---

* Cel., II, 200; Socii, 15. This, too, is indicative of the spirit of chivalry which
animated the Saint that the Saviour and His Mother together were the objects
of his loving homage. This was characteristic of true chivalry: "The devotion to
the Virgin animated and lighted up all our old romances, and the name of Mary
is repeated almost as often as that of her Son." Gautier, *La Chevalerie*, 41.

daily in humble memory of the sufferings of the Saviour." The
actual "dubbing" of the knight took place with the admonition:
"To the honor of the Almighty God I consecrate thee a knight. But
bear in mind how the Saviour of the world was struck for thee
before the highpriest Annas, mocked before Pilate, scourged and
crowned with thorns, clothed with the mantle of derision before
king Herod, jeered at and stripped before all the people, covered
with wounds and was crucified. I recommend to thee to be mindful
of His shame, I counsel thee to take up His cross, and I exhort thee
to avenge His death."[25] Following this admonition, thousands of
knights took up the cross and traversed the seas in order to regain
the holy places for Christ and Christendom. The Crusaders — a
majority of them at least — were animated by so childlike a faith
and so ardent a love for the Passion and death of the Saviour that
today we can hardly realize the depths of their sentiments. But the
chansons, the songs of the Crusades give us an inkling. They know
only two *motifs:* the bitter sorrow of the knight-errant who must
leave his "sweet" homeland and the lady of his heart, and the heroic
urge to risk life and limb for the Crucified. Thus the glorious champions sang: "By God, long enough have we played an indolent
game of knights! Now we go forth, to avenge the cruel ignominy
which must embitter and shame everyone. For in our day the Holy
Land has been lost where God suffered for us and died in the agony
of His soul! If we suffer our archenemies any longer in those places,
our life will be an everlasting disgrace. Whoever does not wish to
dishonor himself shall go to a glorious death for God!"[26] Another
knightly troubadour sang: "O good Lord God, for Thee I leave all
which was near and dear to me, for Thee I lose my heart and my
delight [his lady love]. I devote myself to Thee as Thy vassal,
charming Father Jesus Christ. Nowhere could I find so good a
Liegelord: whoever serves Him, cannot be betrayed."[27] Other Crusaders cried out with deep emotion: "He who was nailed to the
Cross for us did not love us with a false love, but with perfect
friendship. He took the Cross upon Himself out of great tenderness
toward us. Out of pure compassion and with unspeakable meekness
He took it into His arms and pressed it to His heart as a patient,

innocent, and gentle Lamb. Then He let His hands and feet be pierced by three nails and fixed to the Cross. . . . No man can do too much for God the Lord. The mere memory of His death fills my heart with such compassion and faith that nothing can make me fail Him, no matter what I may have left for His sake."[28]

The devotion to the Passion and cross of the Saviour was even more pronounced in the military Orders. In his book *Praise of the New Knighthood* St. Bernard of Clairvaux describes "the greatness and sublimity of the Order of Knights Templar, which was vouch-safed the honor of defending the places where Christ had lived and suffered, and of venerating His Cross."[29] In the oldest statutes of the Teutonic Order the members were called outright "Knights of the Crucified," because "this Order kept in mournful memory the lot of Christ in the ignominy of His Cross and devoted itself to the recovery of the Holy Land, which belongs to the Christians, from the subjugation of the heathens."[30]

Yet never was there a Crusader or Knight so loyal and devoted to the suffering Saviour as Francis of Assisi.

The tragedy of Calvary, the unspeakable pains, the comfortless abandonment, the harrowing death agony of the God-Man most deeply affected the innermost core of his being, took complete hold of all his thought and feeling. Soon after he had become a vassal of the Most High Lord at Spoleto, "Jesus Christ appeared to him one day as if fixed to the Cross, at which sight his whole being seemed to melt away; and so deeply was the memory of Christ's Passion impressed on his heart that it pierced even to the marrow of his bones. From that hour, whenever he thought upon the Passion of Christ he could scarcely restrain his tears and his sighs."[31]

Some time after this occurrence Francis was kneeling before the crucifix at St. Damian's. Then a miraculous thing happened. From the image of the tortured God-Man a voice was heard calling the suppliant Francis to the liege service of the Crucified. "From that hour," writes Celano, "he was pierced with compassion for the crucified Saviour, so that for the rest of his life he bore in his heart the holy wounds, which later were impressed on his body. The sufferings of Christ were always before his eyes and filled them with ever-flowing tears. One heard his weeping everywhere; at the memory of Christ's wounds he was inconsolable."[32]

On another occasion he was walking along the road which leads by the Portiuncula, his voice lifted up in loud lamenting. A certain friend happened to be passing by and asked him what had befallen him. "The sufferings of the dear Saviour," Francis replied. "I weep over the sufferings of the crucified Saviour, and I would fain traverse the whole world thus weeping, without shame, and fill it with the lament over the sufferings of my Lord." He said this with such an overwhelming sense of sorrow that his friend began to weep with him.[33]

Even in his exterior Francis took pains to show himself a knight of the Crucified. He marked a cross, such as the Crusaders and the military Orders wore, on the poor garment given him by the servants of Bishop Guido. The later habit of the Order, too, had the form of a cross, thus to express the love and reverence which the friars were to have for this sacred symbol, as Celano writes: "He wished to clothe himself in the Cross, choosing a garb of penance which set forth its image. Although he chose it because of its poverty, he also desired it to express the mystery of the Cross. He wished his entire body to be clothed with the Cross of Christ, even as his spirit had put on the Crucified, and since God had vanquished the powers of hell in this sign, so also the Franciscan army was to serve its Liege Lord under this standard."[34] Francis himself never used any other seal than the sign of the cross (under the then customary form of the letter *tau* or T). This was the only seal he used on his letters and other writings; even the walls of the cells were marked by him with the figure of the cross.*

Even more: "The entire public and private life of the man of God was centered in the Cross, and from the first moment when he became a knight of the Crucified, various mysteries of the Cross

---

* Cel., *Tract. de mirac.*, 3; Bonav., *Leg. de mir.*, 10, 7. This, too, was in harmony with the customs in vogue at the time of the Crusades. Not only did the illiterates use the cross as a signature, it was placed by everyone as an expression of reverence on letters, documents, and other writings. Voyages were undertaken, battles and even games were begun with this sign. ("*La croix de par Dieu est mise en tête des lettres, des chartes, des alphabets. On inaugure les voyages, les combats, les jeux même par le signe de la croix.*" Gautier, *La Chevalerie*, 34, n. 1.)

began to shine forth in him."[35] Brother Pacificus one day beheld with bodily eyes the sign of *tau* or the cross shining with dazzling splendor on the forehead of Francis. Brother Monaldus one time saw Francis before him fixed to the cross during the time that St. Anthony of Padua was preaching on the mystery of the cross. Brother Sylvester at various times saw a golden cross issuing from the mouth of the Saint, its beam reaching up into the heavens and its arms stretching out unto the ends of the earth.[36] Brother Leo, however, beheld in broad daylight a wondrously beautiful cross moving before the face of Francis, and Christ hanging thereon. When Francis stood still, the cross stood still; and when he moved onward, the cross moved onward also; and whichever way he turned, the cross also turned. And it shone with such brilliancy that its splendor bathed not only the seraphic Saint but all the surrounding countryside, the air, and the earth, in a bright flood of light.[37]

Just as the cross dominated his whole life, so also was his devotion to the cross the dominant characteristic of his life.

Wherever he and his brothers happened to see a cross, they felt themselves to be near the "Tabernacle of the Most High," and they fell down and adored.[38] In his last will and testament the Saint declared: "The Lord gave me such faith in the churches that I would with simplicity adore and say: We adore Thee, most holy Lord Jesus Christ, here and in all Thy churches throughout the world, and we praise Thee, because by Thy holy Cross Thou hast redeemed the world."[39] His predilection for the devotion to the holy cross is most clearly seen in the "Office of the Passion of the Lord," composed by him.[40] It is made up of appropriate Psalms, to which he added special verses and orations. The mere fact that Francis even thought of composing an Office of the Passion is significant. In the early Middle Ages the faithful were accustomed to celebrate the triumph, not the sufferings of the Crucified. He was often represented hanging on the cross with a crown and royal robes. Only after the Crusades was He looked upon as the "Man of Sorrows," and Francis was the first one to go so far as to compose an Office to His Passion. According to his own words, it was "arranged to reverence and recall and praise the Passion of the Lord."[41] A closer examination reveals that it indeed extols the main mysteries of the life of Christ. However, the cross is the focal point of the whole devotion, and even the jubilation over the birth of the Infant ends in the admonition: "Bring your own bodies to the Lord as a sacrifice, and bear His holy Cross and follow His most holy precepts even unto the end."[42]

Francis himself carried out this ideal with chivalrous loyalty and a deep sense of homage. The closer he came to the end of his earthly life, the more burning became his desire to show an ever greater love for his crucified Lord. Two years before his death Providence led him to the lonely heights of Monte Alverna. Here, according to his custom, he began a forty days' fast in honor of St. Michael the Archangel.* More than ever before his soul was flooded with the sweetness of heavenly contemplation, more fervently than ever he longed to know and to accomplish the will of the Most High. At this point it was made known to him that Christ would reveal to him what was the will of the Lord if he opened the book of the Gospels at random. Thereupon he prayed with deep devotion, took the Gospel book from the altar and had his companion, Brother Leo, open it. Three times the latter opened it, and three times their eyes fell upon the story of the sacred Passion. Francis felt assured that before his death he must become *conformed to the Crucified in pain and suffering,* after he had imitated Him in every other respect. Although his health was greatly weakened by his labors and austere penances, he did not flinch, but prepared himself with a valiant and stout heart for his impending martyrdom.

One morning — it was about the feast of the Exaltation of the Cross — he was praying on the slope of Monte Alverna. Suddenly he saw a Seraph with six, fiery, brilliantly radiant wings float down

---

* Francis not only fasted regularly from the feast of the Assumption of Mary to the feast of St. Michael (Sept. 29), but otherwise, too, manifested a special devotion to "this great Prince," as he called him (Cel., II, 197). This is in perfect agreement with his knightly character. The Archangel Michael, together with St. George, was the patron of Christian warriors and of the Orders of knights. In the twelfth century there arose a special Order of knights "of the Wing of St. Michael." See H. Prutz: *Die geistlichen Ritterorden* (Berlin, 1908), 93.

from the heights of heaven. He arrived in rapid flight at the place where Francis was praying, and then between the wings appeared the figure of a crucified man with hands extended so that His body formed a cross; hands and feet were nailed to a cross. Two of the wings reached up over the head, two were extended as if in flight, and two covered the entire body. This vision created in the Saint a riot of feelings, rapturous joy being mixed with the deepest grief. His soul was flooded with joy because Christ in the figure of the Seraph looked upon him so graciously; but the sight of his Beloved being crucified thrust the sword of compassionate grief deep into his heart. He felt that through love he now was to be transfigured into Christ the Crucified. The vision disappeared; yet it left a wondrous glow in his heart, and on his body a no less wondrous impression of the five holy wounds. For immediately there became visible in his hands and feet the marks of the nails, such as he had just seen. His hands and feet were pierced in the middle; in the palms of the hands and on the upper side of the feet the heads of the nails became visible; their points, on the opposite side. The heads of the nails were round in shape and black in color. The points grew out from the flesh and stood apart from the rest of the flesh; they were long, bent back, and, as it were, clinched. The right side, which appeared as if pierced by a lance, was marked by a red scar, from which blood flowed.*

---

* Cel., I, 93–96, 112; *Tract. de mir.*, 4 f.; Bonav., 13, 3; 15, 2. Brother Elias, vicar of the Order, gives a different description of the stigmata in the letter to the friars of the Order reporting the death of the Saint. This description of Brother Elias at first glance seems to be at variance with that of Celano-Bonaventure. The historian, H. Berger, in fact, regards them as irreconcilable and prefers that of Brother Elias. But in spite of this we are inclined to agree with Michael Bihl, O.F.M., who has shown that harmony actually exists between the two reports. Anyone who studies this problem must not overlook the fact that the report of Celano is put forth as that of select eyewitnesses, who were examined under oath in the process of the Saint's canonization. Their dispositions were published by Fr. Pennacchi in *Miscellan. francesc.*, XV (Assisi, 1914), 129–137. The letter of Brother Elias is found in *AA.SS., Oct.*, tom. II, p. 668, n. 649–653; Ed. Lempe, *Frère Elie de Cortona* (Paris, 1901), 70 f.; H. Boehmer, *Analekten zur Geschichte des hl. Franziskus von Assisi* (Tübingen und Leipzig, 1904), 90–92. The article of H. Berger is in *Revue d'Histoire eccl.*, tom. XXXV (Louvain, 1939), 60–70: *La forme des Stigmates de S. Francois d'Assise.* Fr. Bihl's article, *De stigmatibus S. Francisci* is in *Archiv. franc. historic.*, III (Quaracchi, 1910), 425 ff.

Now Francis was crucified with Christ in body and soul. Not only did a seraphic love of God flame within him; like the Crucified he thirsted for the salvation of men. Since the wounds of his feet made it impossible for him to walk, he let himself be carried by a donkey through towns and hamlets in order to encourage all to carry the cross of Christ. To the brothers he also said: "Let us begin to serve the Lord, our God; for until now we have done little." Again the great desire overwhelmed him to perform those first exercises of humility, to nurse the lepers as he had done before, and to flog his weakened members to serve his Lord as formerly.[43] "As a fully tried knight in God's army he desired to challenge the enemy to combat once more, and he hoped to engage him in new battles. With Christ leading him, he planned prodigious deeds of valor and final triumphs over his adversary."[44]

Not content with the violent pains caused by the wounds in his hands and feet by day and by night, he yearned for more sufferings. He would have regarded it as unworthy of a knight of the Crucified if he had, indeed, borne the marks of the cross of Christ and not borne also the full torture of crucifixion. God did, indeed, grant his wish, and in full measure. Soon after the stigmatization his body began to be afflicted with ailments more grievous than he had so far experienced.[45] The first was a very painful disease of the eyes, which did not leave him until his death. This malady called for an almost inhumanly cruel treatment with red-hot irons in the hand of a surgeon, and ended in almost total blindness.[46] Six months before his death his poor Brother Body was so tortured by a number of ills that there was hardly a healthy part to be found. The stomach refused almost all nourishment; feet and legs swelled up enormously; frequent vomiting of blood set in. Emaciation reduced him to mere skin and bones — he was a true figure of woe. He himself confessed that it appeared more difficult to bear these tortures than to suffer any kind of martyrdom.[47]

Moved to tears by the sight of his suffering a simple Brother once said to him: "Father, pray that God may deal more gently with thee, for it seems to me that His hand rests heavier upon thee than is meet." At these words the Saint cried out aloud and said: "If I did not know thy pure simplicity, thy company would be a loathing to me henceforth, for thou hast dared to find fault with God's judgment visited on me." And although almost tortured to death with his long and grave illness he cast himself upon the ground, kissed it, and said: "I thank Thee, O Lord my God, for these my pains, and I beseech Thee, O Lord, to increase them a hundredfold, if this please Thee. This is my delight that Thou dost visit me with pains and dost not spare me; to fulfill Thy holy will is to me overflowing consolation."[48] Celano says beautifully: "Persevering on the Cross he merited to fly upwards to the height of the heavenly spirits. For he had always been on the Cross. . . ."[49]

His vicar and successor, Brother Elias of Cortona, reported the passing of the seraphic Saint with deep grieving, but could not help exclaiming: "I announce to you great joy and most wondrous news. As long as the world has stood such an event has never been heard of, except of Christ Jesus, the Son of God. For not long before his death our Brother and Father appeared as one crucified, truly bearing in his body the five wounds of the Saviour."[50]

Thus all the thinking, striving, doing, praying, suffering, and dying of Francis forms one grand heroic poem. From the day on which he was knighted at St. Damian's until his death at the Portiuncula he served his Liege Lord with heroic fealty and became conformed to the Crucified in every way, as far as this is possible to mortal man. The crucified Lord, on his part, rewarded His heroic Paladin with kingly love, granted him His own blood-red escutcheon, and transformed him into a perfect image of Himself.

That is the great secret of this knight-errant of Christ and his Liege King. It is a mystery so wondrous that it made all Christendom hold its breath, that historians have put it on record with most devout hands. It was a mystery which inspired the minnesinger, Lamprecht of Regensburg, to write these simple, yet stirring, lines:

> Each day with spirit most devout,
> For love of Jesus so benign
> He crucifies himself anew;
> With ever loyal heart he sees
> How Jesus good and merciful
> For us was hanged upon the Cross,

For us was struck those grievous wounds.
Therefore with loving grace Christ marked
Him with His own true print,
As with His kingly coat-of-arms.
He, armed with this most potent shield,
Now dares the devil to engage,
So as no other knight e'er dared.
If any ask what this doth mean,
To him I humbly must avow:
My simple mind it fathoms not.
Yet what this mystery doth reveal
Is that this great and holy man
By Him who rules from Heaven's throne,
Is loved with so great tenderness,
For with the wounds he is adorned
With which the Shepherd on the Cross
All Christendom from sin redeemed.
Christ Jesus, come and comfort us
Unto the honor of Thy holy wounds,
With which this knight Thou didst adorn!
And lead us all to heaven's bliss
With Thy most sweet and holy word!*

---

* Lamprecht von Regensburg, *Sanct Franzisken Leben,* ed. for the first time by Karl Weinhold (Paderborn, 1880), verses 4236–4263. Lamprecht wrote this poem between 1240 and 1255. He was then still a knight in the world, but in this poem he asks God through the prayers of Francis to grant him the grace of conversion as it was granted to Francis. He associated with Brother Berthold of Regensburg and other Minorites (verse 1750 ff.), but it is not certain whether he joined the Order later on. The above verses, written in Old-German, were put in modern German by the author, and into English by the translator.

CHAPTER TEN

The Love of the Knight of Christ for His Lady Poverty

JUST as Francis, the knight-errant of Christ, loved his Lord, so he also loved his Lady Poverty. From the moment in which he had become a vassal of the Most High, he began to court her. From the moment of his knighting by the Crucified, his heart belonged also to the Bride of the cross, as Dante sings:

> . . . and he did make her his,
> Before the spiritual court, by nuptial bonds,
> And in his father's right: from day to day
> Then loved her more devoutly.[1]

He had already passed two years at her side in unspeakable bliss when God confirmed the bond of their love forever.* Francis was attending Mass in the Portiuncula chapel — it was February 24, 1209 — when he heard the Gospel describing the sending of the Apostles: "Preach the message; the kingdom of God is at hand! Cure the sick, raise the dead, cleanse the lepers, cast out devils. Freely you have received, freely give. Do not keep gold, or silver, or money in your girdles, nor wallet for the journey, nor two tunics, nor sandals, nor staff . . ." (Matt. 10:8-10). These words struck his ears like a new revelation. "This is what I desire! This is what I

---

* The episodes of the consulting of the Gospel book have been mentioned before in connection with the apostolate of preaching which Francis chose for himself and his companions, yet we now refer to them again because they were the basis on which rested their life of evangelical poverty. This chapter draws its material to a great extent from *The Ideals of St. Francis,* by Hilarin Felder, O.F.M.Cap. (1925), transl. by Berchmans Bittle, O.F.M.Cap., in which all questions relating to Franciscan poverty are extensively treated on pp. 74-165.

seek! This is what my whole heart craves!" he exclaimed jubilantly. Then he threw away staff and shoes, took a cord in place of the leathern girdle, and fashioned a simple garb for himself out of rough cloth.

Now Francis was truly poor, poor in the sense of the Gospel. "His entire riches consisted from the beginning of his religious life until his death in a habit, a cord and drawers. More he would not have."[2] Carried away by his example, Bernard of Quintavalle, a nobleman of Assisi, joined him and said: "Brother, I will distribute all my earthly goods as you see fit out of love for God, who has given them to me." Francis did not wish to make the decision himself, but replied: "Early on the morrow we will go to the church and learn from the book of gospels what the Lord taught His disciples." On the following day — it was the 16th of April, 1209 — Francis went with Bernard and a third companion, the lawyer Peter Catanii, to the Church of St. Nicholas. After fervent prayers they requested a priest to open the Gospel book three times. The first time they read: "If thou wilt be perfect, go, sell what thou hast, and give to the poor, and thou shalt have treasure in heaven; and come, follow Me" (Matt. 19:21). The second time: "Take nothing for your journey, neither staff, nor wallet, nor bread, nor money; neither have two tunics" (Luke 9:3). The third time: "If anyone wishes to come after Me, let him deny himself, and take up his cross and follow Me" (Mark 8:34).

Francis thanked God for having shown him and his disciples the way of true poverty, and then exclaimed: "Brothers, this is our Rule and our life, and of all those who desire to join our brotherhood. Go, therefore, and do as you have heard." Accordingly they went and gave all their goods to the poor, clothed themselves like Francis, and "lived with him after the manner of the Gospel as revealed to them by the Lord."[3] This was repeated every time a new companion asked to be received into the brotherhood. Francis states explicitly in his *Testament:* "Those who adopted this form of life gave all that they possessed to the poor. And we were content with one tunic patched inside and out (by those who wished), and with a cord and drawers, and we desired nothing more."[4]

"They were so full of joy withal," write the Three Companions, "as if they had found the great treasure in the evangelical field of Lady Poverty, for love of whom they despised all earthly things as dung." They add that wherever the brothers went they rejoiced in the Lord, Francis leading them and singing with a loud and clear voice the praises of God after the manner of the French minstrels, glorifying the goodness of God who had led them to the long sought treasure of the holy Grail of Lady Poverty.[5]

Having tested their new mode of living in evangelical poverty for some time — a period that could be called the joyous springtime of their new life — they journeyed to Rome to obtain the approval of the Pope. "Let us go to our Mother," Francis said, "the Holy Roman Church, and make known to the Pope what God has begun through us, so that we may continue what we have begun, according to His will and precept."[6] He had the new Rule written down "in few and simple words," as he says in his *Testament.* This Rule consisted, with the exception of a few regulations, of the texts of the Gospel relating to poverty heard by him and his companions on the day of the birth of his Order.[7]

Although Francis defended his Rule and his life of poverty with great eloquence, Pope Innocent III nevertheless had grave misgivings, feeling that its observance was humanly impossible.[8] He asked Francis first to seek enlightenment from above in prayer. While the Saint was praying as the Pope had bidden him to do, the Lord spoke to him the following parable: "In a desert there lived a poor, but beautiful woman. A king, filled with admiration for her beauty, desired her for his wife, so that she might bear him children as beautiful as herself. After the marriage had been entered into, many sons were born of their union. When these had grown older, the mother said to them: 'My sons, do not be ashamed, for you are sons of the king. Go therefore to his court, and he will give you all that is necessary.' When they therefore came to the king, he admired their beauty, and seeing their great likeness to himself, he asked whose sons they were. They replied that they were the sons of a poor woman of the desert. The king thereupon embraced them with great joy and said: 'Fear not, for you are my children! If strangers eat at my table, how much more you, to whom the inheritance belongs by right!' He then bade the poor woman to send all her children to the court, so that they might find sustenance there."[9]

After Francis had finished his prayer he returned to "the dear Lord Pope," related to him the parable which the Lord had told him, and added: "Lord Pope, I am that poor woman, whom the Lord has exalted and blessed with sons. The King of kings assured me, however, that He Himself would nurture all the children which He would beget through me. For if He nurtures strangers, He must surely nurture also His own sons. Since God gives temporal goods to sinners that they might provide for their children, He will all the more see to it that the men of the gospel receive that which is theirs by right." At these words all the misgivings of the great Pope vanished; he blessed the undertaking of the Little Poor Man, an undertaking based solely on the loving providence of God.[10]

In this parable of the poor woman, her royal consort, and the princes born of their union, Francis reveals a world of truly chivalrous ideas and sentiments. Out of love for Lady Poverty the Lord of heaven brings forth, ennobles, and sustains the family of the Poverello. For this reason Francis and his disciples fostered "the nuptial association with Lady Poverty, determined to adhere faithfully to her always and everywhere. Free from all earthly cares and accessible only to heavenly consolations, they were unshakeably resolved that no trial should discourage them, no temptation ever sway them, and nothing ever tear them from the embraces of Lady Poverty."[11] When writing his later Rules, Francis was most deeply concerned with this particular point. He was forced, of course, by changing conditions to modify and amplify the primitive Rule; however, "in every Rule he stressed poverty above all else."[12]

Whatever Francis enjoined by his precepts, he himself carried out by his own example. His love for Lady Poverty irradiated his whole life, burned in his heart with an undying flame, and found its way constantly to his lips. He often reminded his brothers of the words of the Gospel: "The foxes have holes, and the birds of the air nests, but the Son of Man has not whereon to lay His head."[13] He warned them repeatedly: "In the same measure as the friars recede from poverty, the world will recede from them; they will seek and shall not find. But if they will hold fast to my Mistress, Holy Poverty, the world will provide for them, for they are given to the world for its salvation."[14]

He was determined to surpass all in being poor. If he happened to meet someone whose garment seemed poorer than his own, Francis would reproach himself and try to imitate the poverty of the other, as if he feared to be outdone in the fight which he waged for his Lady Poverty. One day he met a poor man on the road who had only the most necessary clothing. Francis was deeply grieved and said in a tearful voice to his companion: "The poverty of this man makes me greatly ashamed, because, whereas we have chosen poverty in exchange for great riches, he shines forth therein more brightly than we."[15]

The verses of the Psalms which spoke of poverty, such as: "The needy shall not be always forgotten, nor shall the confidence of the afflicted perish forever" (9:19), and: "See, ye lowly ones, and rejoice, for God hears the poor" (68:34), he sang with greater ardor and more jubilation than the others.[16] He would frequently greet the Spouse of his heart with the words: "O Lady, holy Poverty, may the Lord save thee together with thy sister holy Humility!"[17] In his exuberance he called her now Mother, now Bride, now Mistress. Wherever he was, at home or abroad, he sang her praises, and even in his dreams he saw her beloved figure.[18]

This romance of Francis and Lady Poverty, a romance which is historical in all its elements, is so unique that we have neither thoughts to evaluate it fully, nor sentiments to relive it. We lack the high standards and ideals of the knight, of the minnesinger, of the Saint of Assisi. For Francis poverty was a real Mistress, a Lady, a Queen. He made poverty something concrete, he made it a person, he gave it life. He breathed into its body a living soul. He courted her love and favor, as any lover ever wooed the woman loved and revered by him. He sang the praises of her beauty, her grace and goodness, in a song so bold as hardly ever a troubadour sang the praises of his liege lady. He gave himself to her service so fully and unreservedly as ever a knight served his lady. To her he devoted a love "fine and loyal."* A contemporary and eyewitness, Thomas of Celano, could write of it:

"The blessed Father, as long as he tarried in this vale of tears, despised all treasures of men as worthless. He sought after the highest degree of perfection and therefore embraced poverty with ardent love. Because he saw in her the friend of the Son of God, he wished to be espoused to her, who was shunned everywhere, with undying love. Because he had become the lover of her form (*amator formae ipsius*), he left not only father and mother, but renounced all other things in order to cling faithfully to his Lady and with her to be two in one spirit. He embraced her therefore in chaste love and not even for an hour did he wish to be anything but her spouse. . . . No one can be so avaricious of gold as he was desirous of poverty; no one can guard a treasure so jealously as he guarded this pearl of the gospel. That above all things offended his eye if he saw anything around the friars inside or outside the house which was contrary to poverty. In truth, all his riches, from the foundation of the Order until his death, consisted in a habit, the cord and breeches. More he never possessed. Even his poor garb showed where he had laid up his treasures. For this reason he was merry, carefree and happy; he rejoiced because he had exchanged all perishable riches for a hundredfold."[19]

When death drew near he gathered his last strength to sing his swan song to Lady Poverty in his *Testament*. Then he had himself laid upon the floor and his sacklike habit removed. His superior, or guardian, divining the wish of the dying Poor Man, hastily placed on him another habit and drawers and a covering for the head made of coarse material. This covering had become necessary as a

---

* These were the terms used by the poets to characterize the romances of the knights: "Fine and loyal love — that means vowing worship to the lady, means a love exacting long service, high deeds, feats of valor. Whatever might often be the weakness of the songs of adventure, they bear nevertheless the imprint of this chivalrous and elevated character." (*Fine et loyal amour, cela veut dire l'amour vouant un culte à la dame, l'amour exigeant les longs services, les hauts-faits, les prouesses. Quelle que soit souvent la faiblesse des chansons d'aventures, elles portent néanmoins empreint ce caractère chevaleresque et élevé.*) E. Littré: *De la poésie épique dans la société féodale*, Revue des Deux Mondes (1854), III, 58.

result of an eye operation performed on him shortly before. Then the guardian said to the dying Saint: "Know that this habit with the drawers and the head-covering is lent to you in the name of holy obedience. But that you may know that you have no right of possession over them, I deprive you of the power of giving them to another." At these words the soul of the Saint was flooded with jubilant joy, because he had kept his knightly troth to his Lady Poverty unto the end.[20] After admonishing his sons to do likewise, he died in the arms of his beloved Bride.

> Then the season came that He,
> Who to such good had destined him, was pleased
> To advance him to the meed, which he had earn'd
> By his self-humbling; to his brotherhood,
> As their just heritage, he gave in charge
> His dearest Lady: and he enjoin'd their love
> And faith to her; and, from her bosom, will'd
> His goodly spirit should move forth, returning
> To its appointed kingdom; nor would have
> His body laid upon another bier.[21]
>
> — *Dante*

Truly, a wondrous love for Lady Poverty! So wondrous and so charming that it appeals to us like the romantic mystery plays of the Middle Ages. What is its basis, its essence?

In the first place the love which the knight-errant of Christ bore for poverty must be explained as being the result of his being *called to the liege service of his Lord by the Saviour Himself*. When he was endeavoring to explore the will of God, the Saint, time and again, encountered the texts of the Gospel relating to poverty. Never for a moment did he doubt that this was a genuine revelation made to him, and that the ideal propounded by the Gospel was the specific norm of life for him and his brotherhood. He appealed constantly to this, as for instance in his *Testament*: "After the Lord gave me charge over the brethren, no man showed me what I ought to do; but the Most High Himself revealed to me that I should live after the manner of the Holy Gospel."[22]

To live in poverty meant to him as much as living the *evangelical manner of life*. "They lived after the manner of the gospel, which had been revealed to them by God," the Three Companions attest regarding Francis and his associates.[23] When it was suggested to the Saint that he borrow from the Rules of the other Orders he answered with determination: "I wish that you name unto me no other Rule, neither of St. Benedict, nor of St. Augustine, nor of St. Bernard, nor any other way or form of living save that which has been mercifully shown and given to me by the Lord."* Even in the hour of his death he enjoined the faithful observance of poverty on his brothers, declaring that the Gospel was to be preferred to all other religious Rules.[24] By reason of their poverty Francis designated himself and his disciples simply as "evangelical men."[25]

Persons outside the Order concurred with Francis on this point. "He desires to live according to the form of the holy gospel," was the message delivered by Cardinal John of St. Paul to Pope Innocent III.[26] The famous Cardinal and historian James de Vitry, who became closely acquainted with Francis and his companions in Italy in 1216, and again in the Orient in 1219, testifies: "That is truly the religion of the poor men of the Crucified, the Order of these preachers who are called Friars Minor. They are in truth Friars Minor, and by reason of their clothing and poverty and contempt of the world and humility they surpass all religious of their time. . . . They endeavor so zealously to renew the faith, the poverty and humility of the primitive Church, and to draw the pure waters of the evangelical fountain in the thirst and fire of the spirit, that they, following not only the precepts, but also the counsels of the gospel, strive most faithfully to imitate the life of the apostles, renouncing all their possessions, denying themselves, and, stripped of all, following the poor Saviour."[27]

All this points to the fact that a life of poverty such as Francis lived according to the injunction of God also represented the *highest degree of evangelical perfection*. For it was the basic law of perfection which had come to him from the mouth of the Lord when the

---

* Spec. perf., c. 68. He likewise rejected the suggestion of St. Dominic to merge the newly founded mendicant Orders of the Friars Minor with the closely related Order of Preachers into one. Cf. Cel., II, 150; Spec. perf., c. 43. For the traditions of the Dominicans see Gerard. a Fracheto, *Vitae fratrum*, ed. Reichert (Lovanii, 1896), 10 f.

book of Gospels was opened: "If thou wilt be perfect, go, sell what thou hast, and give to the poor, and thou shalt have treasure in heaven" (Matt. 19:21). Francis accepted these words of God in all the simplicity of his soul and all the glowing ardor of his heart. He said later in reference to Bernard of Quintavalle who joined him soon after this incident: "The first brother whom the Lord gave me was Brother Bernard, who began the perfection of the Gospel and consummated it most perfectly by giving all his goods to the poor."[28] "He never allowed a doubt to arise that this Lady Poverty was the way to perfection for his sons."[29] Because Clare and her daughters faithfully observed poverty, Francis praised them for living "a life according to the perfection of the gospel."[30]

It was not that Francis thought that perfection consisted exclusively in poverty. Besides Lady Poverty he sang the praises of the *entire galaxy of virtues,* which together with poverty were to adorn the soul and bestow on it harmonious beauty; his "Salutation of the Virtues" is witness to this.[31] According to his conception, however, poverty was the foundation and the promoter of all spiritual excellence. When the Brothers asked him which virtue in particular makes one a friend of Christ, he answered, as if revealing the great secret of his heart: "Poverty, my brothers! Know that poverty is the special way to salvation as the promoter of humility and the root of all perfection. Its fruit is manifold, though hidden. Poverty is the treasure of which the gospel says it was hidden in a field; to purchase which a man should sell all that he has, and what cannot be sold should be accounted as nothing in comparison with it."[32] Jacopone da Todi, therefore, in a dialogue between Francis and Poverty, has the latter declare that she never appears without the seven virtues inseparably united to her: love, obedience, humility, continence, chastity, patience, and finally hope, which is the "handmaiden" of the others.[33] Francis actually saw in a vision his much beloved Bride as a most beautiful woman who was bedecked with precious jewels, but at the same time was covered with a poor cloak.[34] Poverty the promotor and protector of every virtuous adornment!

That poverty was the very soul of the *three evangelical counsels* *and of the religious vows* was revealed to him one day in a vision. Three women, perfectly alike in figure, age, and facial features, approached the Saint in a broad plain between Campiglio and San Quirico, bowed low, and greeted him with the words: "Welcome, Lady Poverty!" The lover of poverty was filled with inexpressible joy because there was nothing that pleased him more than to be greeted in this manner. The vision then vanished.[35] St. Bonaventure remarks regarding this vision: "It would seem that these women, so poor and so like one another, signified the beauty of evangelical perfection, which consists in chastity, poverty and obedience, all of which shone forth in the holy man in equal beauty and glory, although he gloried in the privilege of poverty rather than in any other thing."*

This is not hard to understand if it is borne in mind how basic and essential poverty was regarded by Francis. To be without possessions of any kind meant to him to be *completely stripped of everything created and to belong to the Creator alone.* "Holy poverty," he was wont to say, "confounds cupidity and avarice and the cares of the world."[36] "Poverty is that heavenly virtue by which all earthly and perishable things are trod under foot and by which all hindrances are removed so that the spirit of man can unite itself freely to the eternal Lord and God. It makes the soul still tarrying on this earth able to associate with the angels in heaven,"[37] and at the moment of death "to go to Christ detached from all earthly things."[38]

All this leads finally to that consideration which fully explains the chivalrous love of the Saint for his noble Lady Poverty. He saw in her *Christ's own Bride and he loved her for the sake of her divine Spouse.*

Was not Christ most intimately united with her every day of His life? From His throne on high the King of the heavenly hosts stepped down to earth in order to seek out the Queen, Lady Poverty,

---

* Bonav., 7, 6. The theological proof that poverty occupies the first place among the Gospel counsels, and therefore forms the basis for evangelical perfection, is brought forward by St. Bonaventure in his treatise: *De perfectione evangelica*, q. 2, a. 1, Opera ed. Quaracchi, t. V, 127 ff.

who was so shunned and despised by men. And lo! She was awaiting Him impatiently in the stable of Bethlehem, together with the
poor Virgin Mary. She clung to His side all during His life as His
most faithful Betrothed and was praised and cherished by Him
above all things of this world. And when the hour of His extreme
degradation and suffering had struck and even His disciples and
friends had deserted Him, Poverty did not leave Him for a moment.
She remained with Him in revilings and jeerings. She stood by
Him when He was spit upon, scourged, and crowned with thorns.
When He finally hung upon the tree of shame between heaven and
earth, cast off by the earth and abandoned by heaven, she stood
close to comfort Him. And while not even His own sweet Mother
could mount the cross with Him, His dearest Bride Poverty held
Him in her loving embrace until death.*

But after her divine Bridegroom had passed from this earth, there
was no one who took her unto himself with such great and undying
love as did Francis. Of this connubial union Dante sings: .

> Nor aught availed her constant boldness
> Whereby with Christ she mounted on the cross
> When Mary stayed beneath. . . . She, bereaved
> Of her first husband, slighted and obscure,
> Thousand and hundred years and more, remained
> Without a single suitor, till he came.[39]

What the prince of poets expresses in these verses the historian
Thomas of Celano had said long before him: "Francis strove constantly to espouse Poverty with an undying love, because she had
been the consort of the Son of God, but now was an outcast in the
eyes of the whole world. He therefore became her faithful lover, so

---

* This connubial love of Christ and Poverty is described in a form as tender
as it is poetic in the booklet: *Sacrum Commercium,* or *Mystical Nuptials of Blessed
Francis and the Lady Poverty.* It was written a few months after the death of the
Saint (July, 1227) by one of the later generals of the Order, John Parenti, or more
probably John of Parma. The entire allegorical description is placed in the mouth
of Francis. The original Latin text with an Italian translation was published by
Ed. Alenconiensis, O.F.M.Cap.: *Sacrum Commercium B. Francisci cum Domina
Paupertate* (Rome, 1900). Another Italian text from the fourteenth century was
published by Salvatore Minocchi: *Le mistiche nozze di San Francesco e Madonna
Povertà* (Firenze, 1901). An English translation under the title: *The Lady Poverty,*
was made by Montgomery Carmichael (London: Burns and Oates, 1901).

that for the sake of his Spouse he left not only father and mother, but all things of this world."[40]

The Saint formulated his own life's program in the words: "I, little Brother Francis, wish to follow the life and poverty of Jesus Christ, our Most High Lord, and of His Most Holy Mother, and to persevere therein to the end."[41] That explains why he was so deeply stirred when he was asked an alms "for the love of God," or even when he merely encountered a beggar.[42] As Celano says: "In every poor man he saw the Son of our poor Lady."[43] And St. Bonaventure relates that he would often burst into tears when he meditated on the poverty of Jesus Christ and of His poor Mother.[44] The mere thought of the poverty of the Virgin Mother and of her Child brought tears to his eyes. "One day, while he was at table, a friar happened to speak of the poverty of the Most Blessed Virgin, and how the divine Child was so completely despoiled of all things. The Saint forthwith arose from the table with mournful sighs, and ate his bread with tears, kneeling on the bare floor. For this reason, he said, this virtue is the royal virtue, because it was so resplendent in the divine King and Queen."[45] He would then add: "I will not forego the royal dignity which our Lord Jesus Christ assumed when He became poor so that He might enrich us by His poverty and so make the poor in spirit to be kings and heirs of the kingdom of heaven. I will not forego it, I say, for the gift of all the false riches which for a short time are granted."[46]

He also admonished the brothers constantly and forcibly to cherish poverty and hold it in esteem most highly because it was the Bride of the Saviour. He inspired his very first associates to strip themselves of all earthly things for thereby they would be restoring all things to the Lord.[47] This thought also occurs in the Rule of 1221: "Let all the brothers strive to follow the humility and poverty of Our Lord Jesus Christ. . . . And when it may be necessary, let them beg for alms. And let them not be ashamed thereof, but rather remember that Our Lord Jesus Christ, the Son of the living and Omnipotent God . . . was not ashamed, and was poor, and a stranger, and lived on alms, He Himself and the Blessed Virgin and His disciples. . . . Alms is an inheritance and a right which is due to the poor, which Our Lord Jesus Christ purchased for us."[48] In the sixth chapter of the Rule of 1223 Francis sets down these precepts as the unchangeable and fundamental law of his Order: "The friars shall appropriate to themselves nothing, neither house nor place nor anything at all; but as pilgrims and strangers in this world, serving the Lord in poverty and humility, they shall go seeking alms with confidence. Nor ought they to be ashamed, since for our sakes Our Lord made Himself poor in this world. This is that sublime height of most exalted poverty which has made you, my most beloved brothers, heirs and kings of the kingdom of heaven; which has made you poor in temporal things but exalted you in virtue. Let this be your portion which leads into the Land of the Living. Giving yourselves up wholly to this, beloved brothers, never seek anything else under heaven for the sake of Our Lord Jesus Christ."[49]

In reviewing the above, one is seized with amazement and a deep sense of awe before this all-surpassing love of St. Francis for poverty. He reveals himself as a man inspired by God, a man who has conceived the gospel of poverty, and we may say boldly, the theology of poverty and the mysticism of poverty in all its depth and all its soaring sublimity. He stands revealed also as the knight-errant of Christ, as the bravest and most loyal Paladin, who worshiped and loved the Mistress of His Most High Lord just as this Lord loved and worshiped her and because this Lord also loved and worshiped her. He stands revealed, too, as a true minstrel and knightly troubadour who consecrated his heart, his song, and his life to his noble Lady Poverty.

CHAPTER ELEVEN

The Troubadour and Minstrel of God

THE troubadours and minstrels of the Middle Ages played an important and significant part in the society of their time, especially at the courts and at gatherings of knights. It is well known that the young son of Bernardone was fascinated by the "gay science" of these musicians and poets and that he was an ardent devotee of their art. But now he had become a knight of Christ. The worldly life and gay doings of these singers and players were no longer in harmony with the life he had chosen. He renounced this life of worldliness and gaiety forever, but only to become a troubadour and minstrel of God. Nature, temperament, and, above all, grace, compelled him with an unyielding urge to anchor this "gay science" in God, to give it thereby new depth, a new life, and a new spirit.

The art of the troubadours was not called the "gay science" without reason, for a merry and joyful spirit was the basic characteristic not only of the players and poets of the time but of knighthood in general. The ideal of chivalry demanded joyfulness as the first requisite of Christian knighthood.[1] "The newly invested knight must be gay," is the injunction given in an instruction on chivalry; "for this is the handicraft of arms: great clamor in the field, great gaiety at home."[2]

The biographers of Francis accordingly note a growing spirit of joyousness at every step taken by him in following out his calling. In relating the vision which for the first time presaged his calling to spiritual knighthood they add: "From that hour he was filled with such joy that he could no longer contain himself, but was forced to give expression to his interior jubilation in the company of others."[3] They tell us how he began to put his chivalrous devotion to God into action by showing a heroic love for lepers, and they stress the fact that while performing this humanly speaking loathsome and repulsive task he experienced an excessive sense of joy.[4] They relate, too, how his divine Liege Lord soon afterward made clear to him the nature of his spiritual knighthood, and they remark that as a result of this revelation his soul was flooded with an overpowering wave of blissfulness in God.[5]

His whole life was henceforth attuned to this basic note of joy and happiness in God. Thomas of Celano asserts: "The Saint constantly strove to persevere in this jubilation of the heart, to keep ever fresh the unction of the spirit and the oil of gladness. With utmost care he avoided the evil of ill-humor."[6] According to the "Mirror of Perfection" his unceasing endeavor was to keep himself both inwardly and outwardly in a cheerful disposition.[7] When in the company of the Brothers he understood how to remain so joyful and merry that they felt themselves raised to an almost heavenly atmosphere. The same joyful note dominated the association of the Saint with his fellow men. Even his sermons on penance became joyous events and his mere appearance became a festive occasion for all classes of people.[8]

Joyfulness transfigured even his almost ceaseless weeping over the sufferings of the God-Man, and over his, as he thought, countless and grievous sins. St. Bonaventure lays special stress on this particular trait in the character of the Saint: "He never ceased to cleanse his soul in the rain of tears, striving after the purity of supernatural light, and counting as little the loss of his bodily sight. Yet though he shed streams of tears, he was filled with a certain heavenly joyfulness which transfigured his spirit and his face. In the spotlessness of his pure conscience he overflowed with the oil of joy, so much so that his spirit was constantly immersed in God and that he unceasingly rejoiced in the works of the Lord."[9] His own sufferings were suffused by the light of this joy in God. The Three Companions remark: "His heart rejoiced so much in the Lord that his weakened and mortified body became strong enough to endure all hard and bitter things."[10] In the last days of his illness a well-meaning Brother thought it his duty to remind the Saint that the people of Assisi might take scandal at his display of joyousness. Francis quieted him and said with fiery enthusiasm: "Give me leave, Brother, to rejoice in the Lord and in His praises and in my own infirmities, for by the grace of the Holy Spirit I am so joined and made one with the Lord that by His mercy I may well be joyous in Him, the Most High."[11]

It is only natural that this spirit of joy led him to emulate the troubadours and minstrels in their love for *music and song*. But while he and his merry companions had formerly made the streets of Assisi resound with the music of the lute and of gay songs,[12] he now made field and forest resound with the praises of God. "With indestructible equanimity and merriness of heart he sang to himself and raised the song of joy to God," says Celano.[13] Not only in the hours of happiness but also in those of trial and suffering he had recourse to music and song in order to lift up his spirits. At the time when he suffered torments from a malady of the eyes, he called one of the Brothers who had been a lute player in the world and said to him: "Brother, I wish that you would quietly borrow a lute, compose a song for it and thus afford relief to my body which is in great pain." His companion answered: "I fear much, Father, that the people might take this as a touch of frivolity on my part." The Saint then replied: "Then let it be, Brother." While he was lying awake, however, the following night, and had his thoughts centered on God, a wondrously sweet melody suddenly struck his ear. He saw no one, but he heard the music now from here, now from there, as if a lute player were walking back and forth. In the words of Celano, his soul, already firmly fixed on God, experienced in this sweet and melodious music of the angels such heavenly rapture that it seemed as if he were already in paradise.[14]

Those brothers were especially dear to him who were versed in religious music and song. One was Brother Juniper, whose expertness in this regard receives special mention: "Brother Juniper was an excellent troubadour of the Lord, because he often sang of the Lord in flaming words."[15] Brother Giles, too, who despite his simplicity was well acquainted with the *Song of Roland,* also receives high praise: "This holy man was always cheerful and merry. If he spoke with anyone on the words of God, he was filled with marvellous joy. In his boundless rapture he would then kiss straw and stones and do many like things from pure devotion. But whenever he found himself in such astounding grace, it became bitter to him to turn from God to eating. He then wished to live on the leaves of the trees so that he might not lose the grace of conversing with God for even one hour. When he finally again returned to the brothers, he walked along merry and joyous and singing to God, and he said: No tongue can express it, no writing can describe, no man's heart can conceive what God has prepared for those that love Him."[16] Even more significant was the affection which Francis had for Brother Pacificus. This troubadour had lived a "godless life" in the March of Ancona and had composed many lascivious love songs. He was called the "King of Verses," because he charmed the society of his day with his songs, and for this reason he had been crowned by the emperor as poet laureate. Francis met him by chance and invited him with chivalric *courtoisie* to join his band and become a troubadour of God. The "King of Verses" answered bluntly: "Let it be done with few words. Let us pass on to action. Take me from the midst of men and give me back to the great Emperor of Heaven." The next day he was given the habit of the Order and henceforth his harp was attuned to the melodies that spoke of the love of God and the joy in God instead of earthly love.[17] In the company of such nightingales Francis was supremely happy: he urged them to sing and he himself sang with them until his strength failed.[18]

Another thing he had in common with the troubadours and minstrels was the urge for *mimetic expression or dramatic action.*

The *Gaya scienzia* of the troubadours was not content with word and music: it demanded "play," mimicry and dramatic action. The wandering "gleemen" were named minstrels or jongleurs or "players"* precisely because the romantic epics (*chansons de geste*

---

*In Latin, *jocularis* or *joculator;* Provençal, *joglar;* French, *jongleur;* Italian, *giullare.*

or *d'aventure*), love songs, and other pieces in their repertory were accompanied by mimicry and action, were enacted and dramatized, in short: *played*. The part of the troubadours was, strictly speaking, the composing or "inventing" (finding) of verses and music.* Some of them also had the faculty of singing or reciting their own compositions and acting or "playing" them, and for this reason they were called "players."

That the youthful Francis was strongly attracted by the romantic aura which surrounded the troubadours and was drawn to emulate them is well known. However, this urge for acting or playing — the latter has a rather profane connotation but is a fitting term — later on asserted itself so strongly in knightly minded Francis, along natural as well as spiritual lines, as is found in no other devotee of the "gay science."[19] He possessed in a marked degree the instinct for pantomimic delivery, this Italian propensity for gesture and acting which turns small and great events or even mere conversation into dramatic representation. The gay companions of his youth had already been fascinated by it. The prologue to his romance of Lady Poverty was "played" by him before St. Peter's when he begged alms in French, costumed as a beggar.[20] Years later, when he was ill and had eaten some meat during the Lenten season, he had himself dragged to the market place in Assisi, wearing only his drawers and with a rope around his neck. At the same time the Brother who "played" the accompanying role in this "drama" had to cry out again and again: "Look at this glutton, this gorger, who secretly stuffs himself with roast chicken and wants to be looked upon as a Brother of Penance!"[21]

On one Easter feast he "played" the role of a pilgrim. He borrowed a pilgrim's hat and staff, knocked on the door of the friary at mealtime, and begged the friars for a piece of bread *per amore di dio*. When they had admitted him and handed him a small dish of food he placed it in a heap of ashes, sat down beside it, and cried out joyously: "Now I sit here as it becomes a Friar minor."[22] On

---

* From the Old Latin *tropare* (to find, to invent). The poet-composer was therefore called in Latin, *tropator;* in Provençal, *Trobador* or *trobar;* in French, *troubadour;* in Italian, *trovatore, trovere.* The German word *Minnesinger* is restricted to minnesongs or love songs.

another occasion he wanted to represent the Nativity of the Saviour "before bodily eyes" as it had occurred at Bethlehem. His friend, Giovanni Velita, had to prepare a stable with an ox and an ass and a crib in the woods. In the holy night Francis then led a group of friars and simple countryfolk in procession to New Bethlehem. Vested as deacon, Celano writes, "his voice, his strong voice, his sweet voice, his clear and sonorous voice announced in honey-sweet words the birth of the poor King of heaven. . . . But when he said the word 'Jesus' or 'Bethlehem' he let his tongue glide over his lips as if to taste the sweetness of this word with his palate and to relish it." When pronouncing the word "Bethlehem" he could not help imitating the bleating sound of a lamb — in reference to the Lamb of God.[23] Similar dramatizations and symbolic representations occur frequently in the life of the Saint. He possessed such a lively imagination, such a rich gift of expression, such an inexhaustible talent for improvisation, that any little corner became a stage, every object an actor.

This aptitude and bent for "acting" placed its mark also on his preaching. Thomas of Celano writes on this point: "He was a man of unusual eloquence. His face beamed with joy when he began to speak; his expression was full of kindness, his speech meek, fiery and measured, his voice strong, sweet, clear and sonorous. . . . Christ, the true Strength and Wisdom, imparted to his speech power and force."[24] A Bolognese student who heard him preach on the feast of the Assumption, in 1222, reported that "Francis did not speak after the manner of ordinary preachers, but as a popular speaker."[25] Everything in this inspired apostle was life, movement, visual demonstration, so much so that people flocked together not only to hear him but to see him.[26] Thomas of Celano says aptly: "He made his body a tongue."[27] The whole man spoke, and his whole speech became a spectacle. This manner of dramatic preaching was used before simple folk and before learned and highly placed people. On one occasion he preached to the august assemblage of Pope Honorius and his cardinals with such fervor and enthusiasm that he almost lost control of himself. "While his mouth spoke," says Celano, "his feet moved about with the agility of a dancer."[28]

Even when immersed in contemplation Francis remained God's troubadour. Thomas of Celano reports that the interior melody and the sweet movement of the Holy Spirit became audible externally in words of the French tongue,[29] and he adds: "He often took, as we have seen with our own eyes, a piece of wood from the ground, laid it on his left arm, held a bow made of a stick and some cord with his right hand and drew it over the wood like over a string instrument, at the same time moving about and singing songs on the Lord in French. But at times this joyous rapture would end in tears, and his jubilation die out in compassion for the sufferings of Christ."[30]

We need not be amazed at these episodes. Francis made his whole life one great Christ-epic and one overpowering drama, a concrete imitation and re-presentation of the life and Passion of his Lord up to the day of His sacred wounds and His death on the hill of Golgotha.

Because he possessed the gift of vivid imagery and dramatization in so large a measure, Francis must be called a *poet,* regardless of whether there are poems of his extant or not. Competent scholars are of one opinion on this point. H. Boehmer analyzes the *psyche* of Francis with sharp discernment and draws the conclusion: "If actually the vividness, freshness and power of imagination is the chief mark of the poetic gift, then Francis was no doubt a poet. . . . Whoever feels and lives thus is a poet, even if he does not speak in verses and figures."[31] Joseph Goerres thus evaluates the poetic genius of the Saint: "If he had cherished an ambition for the poet's crown, it could hardly have escaped him. Nature had endowed him with such a fullness of spirit and such an ardor of sentiment as it is found in few of the troubadours whose works have come down to us. At the court of the art lover Emperor Frederick, who was himself endowed with every gift of a rich mind, the boldest wish of ambition was attainable for him. What Petrarca, what Dante later on became for Italy, he could have become much earlier for his country, and with the poet's crown the grateful favor of beauty was assured him. But if he was a born poet, he was first and above all a born Saint."[32] Adolph Harnack summarizes his opinion in the words: "Thus out of humility and love he molded his life into a poem — he, the greatest poet of his time."[33] Louis Gillet regards Francis, from the standpoint of the history of art, as the "most marvelous poet that ever lived."* Fr. Alexander Baumgartner, in his monumental work covering world literature, evaluates the merits of St. Francis in behalf of Italian literature in the words: "Just as the Poor Man of Assisi was of incalculable importance for Italian art, so was he also for Italian literature. He has filled it with the wondrous ardor of the purest love of God, has directed it into the channel of a new social import by his love of poverty and of his fellowman, he has led it back from the schoolroom to a childlike and joyous love of nature. Even the most severe *critique* has not been able to dim the poetic charm which irradiated his whole being. . . . His life itself has become a poem. . . . The troubadour of Assisi has most powerfully affected the poetry of the period following him above all by clothing his love of poverty and self-abnegation in the allegory of a nuptial relation and thus creating a species of love-song which in fullness and lyrical sweep, in richness of imagery and in beauty can vie for the palm with the secular love-poetry of his time. He has thus conferred on the entire cultural life of his time a higher and a nobler character."[34]

The question now arises whether Francis sang only the songs of others, or whether *he himself composed such songs*. In the former case he could be called merely a minstrel, in the latter he was at the same time an "inventor," composer, a *trovatore* or troubadour in the strict sense of the word. A way to the solution of this question can be opened by considering the language in which the Saint sang.

In the first place, he and his friars sang the liturgical hymns in the *Latin* language. Proof of this is no longer needed today. The simple recitation of Church prayers was limited mostly to private prayer in the early days of the Franciscan era. At public Church

---

* Despite his high opinion of St. Dominic Gillet says: "St. Dominic does not offer this unheard of blending of sensitiveness and passion, of optimism and tenderness, of a refined aristocracy and popular spirit which makes St. Francis the most marvellous poet that ever lived." *Histoire artistique des Ordres Mendiants* (Paris, 1912), 20.

services, the Mass and the Breviary together with the *Prosae* or Sequences and other metrical and rhymed forms of hymnody then coming into vogue, were performed after the choral method of the Papal Curia.[35] That Francis composed nonliturgical poems in the Latin tongue need not cause any wonder, although he did not master this language fully. It was still quite generally understood in his day and was more readily employed for literary purposes than was its recent offspring, the Italian. In any case, there are two songs extant composed by the Saint in Latin, the *Praises of God,* and the *Salutation of The Blessed Virgin.*

It is not easy to establish just how much Francis composed in one of the Romanic dialects. Just as these were closely related to the Latin mother tongue, so also to each other. In this regard it is significant that Raimbaut de Vaqueiras (died about 1207), who was born in the Provence but spent many years in Italy, was able to deliver a five-language "descort" (a type of lyric in which the stanzas are unlike), each stanza of which was composed successively in the Provençal, the Tuscan, the French, the Gasconian, and the Castilian language.[36] Dante remarks that there existed in Italy, "that little corner of the earth," no less than fourteen idioms, or dialects, and that these were divided into more than a thousand varieties.[37]

Francis no doubt often used the Umbrian dialect and the Provençal language, for the troubadours of his day and country composed their songs now in the Italian, now in the Provençal tongue.[38] On the occasion of an investiture of knights at Monte Feltro, now San Leo in the Romagna, he selected as the theme of his sermon the verses:

Tanto è' il bene ch'io aspetto,
Ch'ogni pena m'è diletto.
(So great the good which I do see,
That ev'ry pain is delight to me.)[39]

They were taken from a profane minnesong and for that very reason were bound to attract the attention of the august assembly of knights and their retinue which had gathered from all parts for the gay and brilliant festivities. Francis, however, spoke so devoutly and so full of the spirit of God that all his hearers were deeply moved and regarded the speaker as an angel.[40] One day, as mentioned above, he requested one of the brothers to compose a "suitable song" and to accompany it on the lute.* This indicates that he took great pleasure in popular songs sung in the vernacular tongue. In fact, we possess one of these which he dictated and set to music and to which he himself gave the name of "The Praises of the Creatures. . . . To the Honor of God," more commonly known as *The Canticle of the Sun.* In connection with this the "Mirror of Perfection" reports that Francis composed a similar poem together with its musical setting for the Poor Ladies of the Convent of St. Damian. Unfortunately it has not survived.**

His favorite language, however, was French. Even as a youth "he delighted in speaking French, although he did not know how to speak it faultlessly," the Three Companions report.[41] It was in French that he begged for alms before the Church of St. Peter in Rome, and again in French that he asked for contributions to rebuild St. Damian.[42] After his espousals with Lady Poverty he sang the praises of God's goodness through field and forest in the French tongue.[43] On his first missionary journey into the March of Ancona he jubilantly sang in French "the praises of God with a loud and clear voice and extolled the goodness of the Most High."[44] Even when carried away by ecstasy he sang to the Lord in the French tongue.[45] In all moments of extraordinary devotion and inspiration he gave vent to his feelings in the French language.

How is this unusual enthusiasm of the Saint for the French tongue to be explained? In the first place, knighthood and knightly doings and ways were indigenous to France. Then, too, the French tongue was generally regarded by the Italians as the most fluent and

---

* "I would wish, Brother, that you borrow a lute and bring it here and on it make a suitable song in order to give some solace to Brother Body so full of pain." *Vellem ergo, frater, ut secreto citharam mutuatus afferres, qua versum honestum faciens fratri corpori doloribus pleno solatium aliquod dares.* Cel., II, 126.

** "*Postquam beatus Franciscus fecit Laudes Domini de Creaturis, fecit etiam quaedam verba cum cantu pro consolatione et aedificatione Pauperum Dominarum. . . .*" Spec. perf., c. 90. (After the Blessed Francis had composed the "Praises of the Creatures" he also composed certain words with music for the consolation and edification of the Poor Ladies.)

pleasing popular idiom.* The French hero epics were in fact written in this language and delivered in it throughout Italy by the troubadours. These epics of chivalry fired the enthusiasm of the Assisian knight-errant of Christ all the more since the heroic paladins appearing in them, especially in the *Song of Roland,* were fighters and martyrs for the faith.**

Thus it is understandable that in the life of Francis traces are constantly found of the great French epics. Because he himself was a poet, his life, too, was inspired by the noblest of poetry. Even though he was a troubadour and minstrel of God, yet he evidently leaned heavily on the French *chansons de geste.* These stimulated him in particular, as will be seen, to compose hymns of praises to God. Nevertheless it is not probable that he composed songs in French. Certainly none have been handed down.***

It will not be too difficult then to establish *which songs were com-*

---

* Dante, *loc. cit.,* designates the "Lingua oïl" as the most widely spread "on account of its easier and more pleasing common usage" (*propter sui faciliorem ac delectabiliorem vulgaritatem*). For this reason other Italian writers of this period also composed their works in the French language, for instance, Brunetto Latini wrote his Encyclopedia (under the title "Trésor") in French because this tongue was "more pleasing" (*plus delitauble*); Martino da Casale used French for his Venetian Chronicle because it was more "delitable" than other languages. See Gaspary, *Storia della letteratura Italiana,* I, 107 f. Also G. Bertoni, *Il Duecento,* 47 ff.

** "All this literature is born in the shadow of the cloister. . . . These poems of chivalry were even then lives of the saints, hagiographies thinly disguised. . . . It is very plain that Roland, Oliver, Turpin, are martyrs. Ogier the Dane, William of Orange, Renoud of Montauban are all persons occupied with accomplishing their salvation under tragic conditions. It can be said of them all what the poet writes of one of them: 'Such great things he did on earth that he is crowned in Heaven.' Heroism and sanctity are here the same: the two are fused; one scarcely discerns the nuance that separates the two states, the world strictly human from the world of grace. These two worlds interpenetrate at all times, one floods the other in poetry as well as in life; and this is what constitutes the grandeur of those old epics and their profound moral beauty." Gillet, "Sur les pas de S. François," in: *Revue des Deux Mondes,* 7. periode, t. 34, 754.

*** M. Beaufreton, *S. Francois d'Assise* (Paris, 1925), 7 f. and J. Salvat, *S. François et les Troubadours* (Orien X, Toulouse, 1926) assume without basis that one must think of Provençal love songs when it is mentioned that Francis often sang in French. The Provençal idiom was regarded no more as French than the Italian or Spanish. Besides, the source texts which are evidence of the love of Francis for France and the French people as well as for French songs and the French language, allow us to think only of northern France and the kingdom of France, and of the *language d'oïl.* In order to be convinced of this one need read only Cel., I, 120.

posed by Francis. St. Bernardine of Siena was the first to ascribe to him the two poems: *In foco l'amor mi mise* and *Amor di caritade.*[46] He had discovered them among old manuscripts, found Franciscan ideas in them and forthwith named Francis as their author. Nobody doubted this assumption until it was shattered by Fr. Ireneo Affò in 1777.[47] Nevertheless they were repeatedly ascribed again to the Troubadour of Assisi during the nineteenth century and several strophes were added.[48] Today nobody would think of ascribing these songs to St. Francis.[49]

But neither would anyone think of doubting the genuineness of the three canticles to which he himself gave the titles of *The Praises of God, Salutation of the Blessed Virgin,* and the *Canticle of the Sun.* Besides these three the Saint composed other literary pieces which bear the character of spiritual poetry. Among these is his *Salutation of the Virtues,* that is of "Queen Wisdom" and her "Sister, holy pure Simplicity," of "Lady Poverty" and her "Sister, holy Humility," of "Lady holy Charity" and her "Sister, holy Obedience," and of the entire brilliant retinue of virtues.[50] Mention must also be made of the poetically inspired Paraphrase or gloss-song of the Our Father and the "Lauds" or Praises appended to it, which he said at all canonical Hours of the day and night and also before the Office of the Blessed Virgin Mary.[51] Attention must be called also to many passages in his *Letters,* which were dictated by his ardent zeal;[52] to those parts of the "Office of the Passion" of which he was the author,[53] and to the twenty-first chapter of the First Rule: "Of the Praise and Exhortation which all the Brothers may make."[54] However, only the *Praises of God, The Salutation of the Blessed Virgin,* and the *Canticle of the Sun* can be classed as canticles in the strict sense of the word.

Even these cannot be regarded as monuments of rhymed and metric Latin literature, such as flourished in his days, nor as the products of lyric poetry as found at various courts and as cultivated by the Provençal poets and later also by the Italian troubadours. Poetry is not bound to a definite idiom, nor to meter and rhyme. It speaks all languages and clothes itself in prose as well as in versified form. The *Praises of God, The Salutation of the Blessed Virgin,* and the *Canticle of the Sun* of the Poor Man of Assisi are pearls of religious lyric poetry, although the former two are written in plain Latin prose, and the latter consists of simple assonant strophes written in the Italian idiom then coming into existence.[55] They help us penetrate into the poetically inspired world of prayer and sentiment of St. Francis; they are a true mirror giving us a lifelike picture of the poetic soul of the Troubadour and Minstrel of God.

Praise of God

That the praise of God is essentially important in the life of the Christian and especially of a saint goes without saying. However, in the Poverello it assumes such a wide range and such a distinct form as it is hardly found elsewhere in hagiography. Furthermore, it is noteworthy that in the case of Francis the praise of God always sought expression in the French tongue. The influence and stimulation on the part of the Carolingian hero epics is indicated here as in all his songs in general. Just as the composers of the *chansons de geste* and with them the wandering minstrels sang the praises of Charlemagne and of the valorous deeds of his paladins, so also the knight-errant of Assisi was driven to sing the praises of his sovereign Liege Lord before all the world.

Hardly had he been called to the rank and service of a knight of Christ when he began "to make the forests resound with the praise of the Creator sung in a mighty voice and in great joy of spirit."[56] Soon afterward he appeared in his native city and "sang in the streets and public places the praise of God as if drunk in the spirit."[57] On various occasions Bernard of Quintavalle observed how he passed whole nights "praising God and the Most Blessed Virgin and Mother."[58] Moved by this spectacle Bernard joined the company of the man of God and distributed his goods to the poor, while Francis praised and extolled the Lord.[59] A little while afterward Francis set out on his first missionary tour to the March of Ancona in company with Brother Giles. Both "were loudly jubilant in the Lord, and the holy man praised and glorified the goodness of the Most high, singing with a loud and clear voice songs of praise in the French tongue."[60] It would lead too far afield to demonstrate that the *entire ensuing life of Francis was attuned to the singing of the praises of God.*

His prayer life also was an almost unbroken song of God's praises. All his exercises of devotion in one way or another flowed into the one mighty stream of the praise of the Most High.[61] He had composed a Paraphrase to the Our Father, the underlying tone of which was again the praise of God. He added special "Praises" or Lauds to the Our Father, in which the whole ardour of his loving soul is revealed. This "Paraphrase of the Our Father" with the "Praises" was recited by the Saint day and night at all Hours of the divine Office and of the "Office of the Blessed Virgin."[62] Whenever he was rapt in ecstasy, as it often happened, the Brothers were to praise God in the meantime and pray to the Lord for him.[63]

For he had trained his Brothers likewise to the praising of God. In the very first hour, when there were hardly twelve of them and they were being led by him to the pope in Rome, he commanded them that on the way "they were to speak only of the praise and glory of God and the salvation of souls."[64] He constantly stressed that the conduct of the Friars Minor be always such that it became a praise of God and an incitement to others to praise Him.[65] One time he wrote a letter in an open field to the Brothers in France, exhorting them to rejoice and to sing the praises of the divine Trinity: "Let us bless the Father and the Son with the Holy Spirit."[66]

Like himself, the Brothers were to be *apostles of the praise of God among the people.* In the Rule of 1221 he placed certain exhortations on the praise of God which all the friars were to address to the people. They were to call out the summons: "Fear and honor, praise and bless God, give thanks and adore the Lord God Almighty in Trinity and Unity, Father, Son, and Holy Spirit, the Creator of all. . . . Let us all, everywhere, in every place, at every hour, and at all times, daily and continually believe truly and humbly, and let us hold in our hearts, and love, honor, adore, serve, praise and bless, glorify and exalt, magnify and thank the Most High and Supreme, Eternal God, who . . . is blessed, praiseworthy, glorious, exalted, sublime, most high, sweet, amiable, delectable, and always wholly desirable above all forever and ever."[67]

In 1223, he wrote a letter to all the Custodes of the Order in which he commanded them: "You shall so announce and preach His praise to all peoples that at every hour and when the bells are rung, praise and thanks shall always be given to the Almighty God by all the people throughout the whole earth."[68] In the fall of 1224, his poetic soul soared to the greatest heights when he wrote the deeply stirring canticle which comprises all that has been said above and therefore can be called the *Praise of God* in the emphatic sense of the word. He had just received the heavenly favor of the stigmata, the marks of the Crucified. A sense of boundless gratitude flooded his heart and forced itself to his lips. He had Brother Leo hand him a sheet of parchment and on it he wrote a *"Te Deum* than which a more glowing one has never been sung."[69]

Tu es sanctus Dominus Deus solus, qui facis mirabilia.

Thou art holy Lord God alone, who workest wonders.

Tu es fortis. Tu es magnus. Tu es altissimus.

Thou art strong. Thou art great. Thou art most high.

Tu es Rex omnipotens, tu Pater sancte, Rex coeli et terrae.

Thou art the almighty King, Thou art the holy Father, King of heaven and earth.

Tu es trinus et unus Dominus Deus, omne bonum.

Thou art the Lord God, Triune and One, all good.

Tu es bonum, omne bonum, summum bonum, Dominus Deus, vivus et verus.

Thou art good, all good, highest good, Lord God, living and true.

Tu es caritas, amor.

Thou art charity, love.

Tu es sapientia.

Thou art wisdom.

Tu es humilitas.

Thou art humility.

Tu es patientia.

Thou art patience.

Tu es securitas.

Thou art security.

Tu es quietas.

Thou art quietude.

Tu es gaudium et laetitia.

Thou art joy and gladness.

Tu es iustitia et temperantia.

Thou art justice and temperance.

Tu es omnia divitia ad sufficientiam.

Thou art all riches to sufficiency.

Tu es pulchritudo.

Thou art beauty.

Tu es mansuetudo.

Thou art meekness.

Tu es protector.

Thou art protector.

Tu es custos et defensor.	Thou art guardian and defender.
Tu es fortitudo.	Thou art strength.
Tu es refrigerium.	Thou art refreshment.
Tu es spes nostra.	Thou art our hope.
Tu es fides nostra.	Thou art our faith.
Tu es magna dulcedo nostra.	Thou art our great sweetness.
Tu es vita aeterna nostra, magnus et admirabilis Dominus Deus Omnipotens, misericors Salvator.	Thou art our eternal life, great and admirable Lord God, almighty, merciful Saviour.*

Francis persevered in singing the praises of God until the end. When his bodily sufferings became almost unbearable, his spirit became always more resigned to God, always more one with God, always more joyous in God. In his last days he continuously sang the praises of God and he constantly urged the brothers to praise and bless the Lord. He also called upon all other creatures to praise God and to love God, and he asked to have the *New Canticle of the Praise of the Creatures of the Lord* sung again and again,[70] that magnificent canticle which he had composed in his long hours of suffering.[71] Unto the very end he remained a troubadour and minstrel of God to whom the very essence of spiritual knighthood was above all else a real crusade for the praise and glory of his Lord.

In fact, with him arose that popular religious form of poetry and that popular religious movement which were connected with the term "praises" (*laude*) and "praisers" (*laudesi*) in the thirteenth and fourteenth century. The *laude* were alternate chants after the

---

* *Chartula* quam dedit fratri Leoni, *Opusc.,* 124 f. This precious sheet, which contains also the blessing of St. Francis to Brother Leo, is preserved to this day in a reliquary in the Sacro Convento at Assisi; the text, however, has suffered because Brother Leo, according to the wish of the Saint, carried the sheet on his person during his life (he died in 1271). Leo added the annotation: "Blessed Father Francis two years before his death kept a Lent in the place of Mount La Verna in honor of the Blessed Virgin Mary, the Mother of the Lord, and of Blessed Michael the Archangel, from the feast of the Assumption of the holy Virgin Mary until the September feast of St. Michael. And the hand of the Lord was laid upon him; after the vision and speech of the Seraph and the impression of the Stigmata of Christ on his body, he made and wrote with his own hand the 'Praises' written on the other side of the sheet, giving thanks to the Lord for the benefits conferred on him." Cf. *Opusc.,* ed. Lemmens, 198–200; Boehmer, *Analekten,* LIX; P. Robinson, *Writings of St. Francis,* 146 ff.; also Cel., II, 49.

manner of the former liturgical responsories. The text of the *lauda* was sung by a single cantor or by a group and then repeated or answered by the people in common, somewhat in the form of a dialogue. The Franciscan composers of the *laude* accomplished incalculable good, although with the exception of Jacopone da Todi few of them are known. Their songs became common property, as it usually happens with popular songs.* Wherever the Brothers Minor appeared, they gathered the people about them and alternately sang with them the praises of the Lord.** At countless devotional gatherings in churches as well as in the open the melody of these *laude* rose on high, either in Latin or more frequently in the vernacular. They set in motion a mighty wave of spiritual renewal, one that took hold first in Umbria and Tuscany, and soon after also in most of the other Italian provinces. The impetus of this reform wave carried it even beyond the Alps.***

---

* "The names of the oldest *laudesi* are forgotten. Their poetry became common property, much the same as popular songs. Only one of them is well known to us, a man who in a certain sense has become the personification of the whole group, to the extent that the songs of others have sometimes been ascribed to him: he is Fra Jacopone da Todi." Gaspary, *Storia della letteratura italiana, loc. cit.,* 140. Cf. A. D'Ancona, *Jacopone da Todi, il giullare di Dio del sec. XIII* (Todi, 1914). The best collection of the *laude* of Jacopone was already made by Francesco Bonaccorsi, *Laude di frate J. da Todi* (Firenze, 1490). A new edition was published by G. Ferri, Bari; 2 ed., riveduta da S. Caramella (Bari, 1930). Regarding these *laude* or hymns see also Father Cuthbert, O.F.M.Cap., *The Romanticism of St. Francis,* p. 185 f.

** An interesting proof of this is found in the so-called *Legenda antiqua S. Francisci* of the Cod. 1046 of Perugia, ed. P. Ferdinand M. Delorme, O.F.M., *Archiv. franc. hist.,* XV (1922), 292: "For often when the friars in the place called Grecio praised the Lord late in the day, as the friars were wont to do in many places at that time, the people of that village, large and small, went out and stood in the road before the village, answering the friars with a loud voice: Praised be the Lord God! so that even the children, who did not as yet know how to speak well, when they saw the friars praised the Lord as well as they could." (*Nam saepe cum in sero fratres de loco [de Grecio] laudarent Dominum, sicut fratres in multis locis illo tempore solebant facere, homines illius castri, parvi et magni, exibant foras stantes in via ante castrum, respondentes fratribus alta voce: Laudatus sit Dominus Deus! ita quod etiam pueri nescientes adhuc bene loqui, cum viderant fratres, laudarent Dominum sicut poterant.*)

*** Entirely different from the *laude* and *laudesi* of the Franciscan Order are those of the Flagellants, which appeared from 1260 on, and at first were imbued with a serious pathos, but finally degenerated into frivolous lyric poetry and ultimately sank to the low level of absurdities. The contrast between Franciscan lyric poetry

The Salutation of Mary

Besides singing the praises of God the *laudesi* also sang the praises of the Blessed Virgin Mary.[72] Francis was the model in this movement as well as in the *laude* movement in general. He had always been imbued with a "fervent devotion to the most loving Mother" and "Mistress of the world."[73] His joy was truly childlike whenever he saw her honored. "Rightly," he said, "such great honor is given the Virgin Mary, because she has borne the Lord in her most sacred womb." Next to Christ, he placed all his confidence in her.[74] The homage which he rendered to the Mother of Christ was so inexpressibly deep because, as he was wont to say, she had made the Lord of majesty our Brother.[75] To her he confessed his daily faults and through her he hoped for the forgiveness of the sins supposedly committed by him.[76] He never failed to recite her Office.[77] Besides this, Thomas of Celano assures us, "he dedicated to the Mother of Jesus special canticles of praise (*laude*), addressed special prayers to her, and breathed so many and such tender aspirations of love to her that no human tongue is able to describe it."[78] He spent entire nights in the praise of God and of the glorious Virgin.[79] Every Hour of his Office of the Passion began and ended with the Antiphon: "Holy Virgin Mary, there is none like unto thee born in the world among women, daughter and handmaid of the Most High King, the heavenly Father! Mother of our Most Holy Lord Jesus Christ, Spouse of the Holy Ghost, pray for us with St. Michael the Archangel, and all the Powers of heaven, and all the Saints, to thy Most Holy Son, our Lord and Master."[80]

Still more tenderly and charmingly does he give voice to his love for his dear Lady in his *Salutation of the Virgin:*

---

and that of the Flagellants is tersely characterized by G. Bertoni, *Il Duecento* (Milano, 1911), p. 126: "Franciscan poetry, of which St. Francis himself, Thomas of Celano, Jacopone da Todi and Bonaventure are the more prominent exponents, rises above that immense 'laudistic' flood which poured out impetuously upon a great part of Italy along with the spread of the masses of Flagellants, and assumes an undeniably artistic value together with the deep significance which it has as a phenomenon of history. It was a lyric poetry in Latin and in the vernacular and left conspicuous monuments in literature. . . . "

Ave Domina sancta, regina sanctissima, Dei Genitrix Maria! Quae es Virgo perpetua, electa a sanctissimo Patre de caelo!

Hail, holy Lady, most holy Queen, Mother of God, Mary! Who art ever Virgin, chosen from heaven by the most holy Father!

Quam consecravit cum sanctissimo dilecto Filio et Spiritu Paracleto! In qua fuit et est omnis plenitudo gratiae et omne bonum! Ave palatium eius! Ave tabernaculum eius! Ave domus eius! Ave vestimentum eius! Ave ancilla eius! Ave mater eius! Et vos omnes sanctae virtutes, quae per gratiam et illuminationem Sancti Spiritus infundimini in corda fidelium, ut de infidelibus fideles Deo faciatis!

Whom He has consecrated with the most beloved Son and the Spirit, the Paraclete! In whom was and is all the fullness of grace and all good! Hail, thou His palace! Hail, thou His tabernacle! Hail, thou His house! Hail, thou His garment! Hail, thou His handmaid! Hail, thou His Mother! Hail, all ye holy virtues which by the grace and illumination of the Holy Ghost are infused in the hearts of the faithful, that from unbelievers you may make them believers in God![81]

The *Salutation of Mary* of St. Francis bears the character of a *lauda* just as does his *Praises of God.* As the latter is closely related to the *chansons de geste,* so is the former to the minnesongs of the troubadours, but in an entirely different manner. The hero epics were themselves filled with religious idealism and led directly to the popular *laude* or praises of the Most High. The lyric poetry of the troubadours, however, in which the praises of womanhood were sung, was dedicated to earthly beauty and degenerated more and more into frivolity and even licentiousness. To this poetry Francis opposed the homage and praise of the Virgin Mary, and together with his Order he furthered the popular Marian cult, thus being instrumental in raising the love song to a higher and nobler plane. Around the middle of the thirteenth century the so-called "new and sweet poetry" began to flourish in which a supernaturally transfigured ideal of womanhood was glorified, which showed bright rays of the newly awakened cult of Mary, and was influenced by the Franciscan spirit.* It had its rise with Guido Guinizelli of Bologna

---

* "In the woman who is extolled in the new poetry there is as it were a heavenly

and led through the Brothers Minor Giacomino of Verona and Jacopone da Todi directly to Dante Alighieri.* Already in the works of Guido Guinizelli (1230–1276) the lady whose praises are sung is no longer conceived as a poetically inclined feudal mistress and as the object of sensual desire, but as an angelic creature whose favor ennobles the suitor, places him beyond the realm of everything unworthy and leads him to God.[82] In the poetry of Giacomino da Verona (about the middle of the thirteenth century) the cult of woman becomes definitely the cult of the Virgin Mary. Mary is his Mistress, to her he dedicates his songs, not to earthly women as other poets do. In his poem *The Heavenly Jerusalem* he gives a description of paradise in which this is represented as a brilliant court peopled with knights, at which the Blessed sing the praises of the Queen of Angels and like the troubadours are rewarded with precious gifts.[83]

Jacopone da Todi (1230–1306) it was, who finally became in full measure the *meistersinger* of the Queen of heaven. His Madonna songs are endowed with a charming simplicity, naïveness and popularity of tone. At the same time they are notable for being completely dedicated to Christ. The poet always concludes his reflections on the teaching, suffering, and glorified Saviour with a love greeting to Mary, and whenever his song rises in praise of Mary she is conceived only as a background for the Incarnate Word; her life is a still life for and with Jesus; she is wholly hidden in God, so near to God that her personality is almost lost in His.[84] Jacopone is the greatest representative of the poetry of *lauds*. In his works the seed planted by Francis — the praise of God and of the Blessed Lady — ripened into the choicest fruit.[85]

---

reflection, and in the idealization of woman in the sweet style of poetry there is furthermore a ray of the cult of Mary, which at that particular time was being revived in the West. . . . This more or less light tendency to mysticism drew its nourishment from an unmistakable Franciscan movement which stirred in the depths of the soul." G. Bertoni, *Il Duecento,* 168.

* The former was called by Dante himself "Maximus Guido" (*De vulgari eloquentia,* lib. 1, c. 15), and his master in composing the "sweet and pleasant rhymes of love" (*dolci e leggiadre rime d'amore*). Purgatory, Canto XXVI. Giacomino and Jacopone "can in some measure be regarded as the forerunners of Dante" (Baumgartner, *loc. cit.,* VI, 94).

The Canticle of the Sun

The *Canticle of the Sun* is the cradlesong of the Italian language.*
It is its most precious primitive document and the most brilliant
jewel of religious poetry in the vernacular.[86] But that is not the
point. Just as we revere in Francis not merely the troubadour but
the troubadour and minstrel of *God,* so also his *Canticle of the Sun*
is esteemed not merely as a literary creation but as "The Praises of
the Creatures" sung to God. To him belongs the immortal distinction, even from a purely historical standpoint, of having looked
upon nature with the eyes of a poet deeply imbued with faith, of
having loved it with the heart of a child of God, and of giving to
it a soul and a voice with which to praise the Lord in a thousand
tongues.

The *Canticle of the Sun* did not spring from a momentary emo-
tional movement, but is in truth one of the great events of his
Christian knighthood. We know that Francis sang the praises of the
Lord from the very beginning and that he challenged all men to
join him in this praise. Soon he invited also the irrational creatures
to praise their Creator. With the simplicity of a dove and with un-
precedented ardor of piety he encouraged all elements and all living
things to praise and bless the Author and Preserver of the world.[87]
Wherever he found a meadow bedecked with flowers, he preached
to them and begged them to sound the praises of the Lord, just as
if they possessed reason. The fields of grain, too, and the vineyards,
rocks, and woods; the smiling lea, the verdant fields, earth, fire, air,
and wind — all were called upon by him in the simplicity and sin-
cerity of his heart to serve God, to love Him and to praise Him.[88]

The animals were to be all the more zealous in this matter since
they had been more greatly endowed by their Maker. In this regard
it is significant that the minstrel of God chose above all other creatures the feathered singers as his friends: the falcon who called him
to Matins;[89] Sister Cricket who joined her chirping to his singing;[90]

---

* Ernesto Monaci, to whom we owe the best chrestomathy of the first centuries,
has indeed found older pieces of prose in this language, but no earlier poetry.
See his *Crestomazia italiana dei primi secoli,* Città di Castello (1912), 29–31.

the Sisters Swallows, who seconded his preaching of the word of God just a little too boisterously;[91] the Sisters Doves, Crows, and Jackdaws, who listened so reverently to his sermon: "My feathered Sisters, you especially ought to praise and love your Creator, because He has given you down for your raiment and wings for flight. Among all the creatures God has made you most wonderfully and has allotted the pure air for your element. You neither sow nor reap, and in spite of this He protects and guides you without the least care on your part."[92]

Wherever Francis came in touch with nature he bound it up with his praise of God. Many times, when he was passing through the country and was meditating on God or singing His praises, he would wander from his path and call upon all creatures to raise up their song of praise.[93] Not content with this he wrote "to all Christians, religious, clerics and laics, men and women" the inspired and rapturous words: "Let every creature which is in heaven and on earth and in the sea and in the deep, render praise, glory and benediction to God; for He is our strength and power, He, who alone is good, alone most high, alone almighty and wonderful, glorious and alone holy, praiseworthy and blessed forever and ever in all eternity."[94]

Now he was drawing near the end of his knightly service. It was two years before his passing. Threatened with blindness and tortured with unspeakable pains he was wrestling one night in impassioned prayer for the grace of knightly valor unto the end. Suddenly he heard in spirit the assurance given by the Emperor of Heaven: "Be of good cheer, Brother, and rejoice in thy weakness and tribulations, and be of such confidence as if thou hadst already entered into My kingdom!"* The following morning his spirit soared to the loftiest heights and composed the *Praises of the Creatures,* in which he inspires them to praise the Creator.[95] And because the sun was the fairest of all creatures and because the Lord Himself was called the "Sun of Justice" (Mal. 4:2), he named his swan song

---

* It is fully in accord with the language of chivalry that Francis again and again and up to the time of his death places the emperor at the head of knighthood and the Emperor of heaven at the head of the knights of God.

The Song of Brother Sun.[96] He then taught his brothers "to say and to sing the new *laud.*" He also sent for Brother Pacificus, the one-time "King of Verses" and "most courtly Doctor of song," and commanded him to go with several Brothers throughout the world preaching and singing this *laud.* The one that "knew best how to preach was first to announce the word of God unto the people, and after the preaching all should sing together the Song of the Sun as if they were minstrels of the Lord. And when the Praises were ended . . . the preacher was to say to the people: We are the minstrels of the Lord, and this reward we ask of you that you remain in the state of repentance!" Francis then added: "For what are the servants of God but certain minstrels of His that thus lift up the hearts of men and move them to gladness of spirit?"[97]

A short time after this he heard that a grave dissension had broken out between the bishop and the podestá of Assisi. He immediately added to the *laud* the stanza of forgiveness and peacefulness, asked the dissidents to appear in the court of the bishop's palace, and had the *Canticle of the Sun* sung in their presence. Hardly had the last notes died away when the bishop and the podestá fell into each other's arms and with tears kissed each other as a sign of lasting peace and harmony.[98]

A few days before his death, "hearing that Sister Death was close at hand," he was overcome by "a new gladness of mind, and with great fervency of spirit he gave praise unto the Lord," and he cried out: "Forasmuch as it pleases the Lord that I am soon to die, call Brother Angelus and Brother Leo unto me that they may sing to me of Sister Death." They came, and "full of grief and sadness and with many tears they sang the Song of Brother Sun and of the other Creatures of the Lord." Before they came to the end of the song, the Saint added the second and third last stanza on "Sister Death."[99]

> Most high, omnipotent, good Lord,
> Praise, glory and honor and benediction all are Thine.
> To Thee alone do they belong, most High,
> And there is no man fit to mention Thee.
> Praise be to Thee, my Lord, with all Thy creatures,
> Especially to my worshipful Brother Sun,

The which lights up the day, and through him dost Thou bright-
ness give;
And beautiful is he and radiant with splendor great;
Of Thee, Most High, he signification gives.
Praised be my Lord, for Sister Moon and for the Stars,
In heaven Thou hast formed them clear and precious and fair.
Praised be my Lord for Brother Wind
And for the air and clouds and fair and every kind of weather,
By the which Thou givest to Thy creatures nourishment.
Praised be my Lord for Sister Water,
The which is greatly helpful and humble and precious and pure.
Praised be my Lord for Brother Fire,
By the which Thou lightest up the dark.
And fair is he and gay and mighty and strong.
Praised be the Lord for our Sister, Mother Earth,
The which sustains and keeps us
And brings forth diverse fruits with grass and flowers bright.
Praised be my Lord for those who for Thy love forgive
And weakness bear and tribulation.
Blessed those who shall in peace endure,
For by Thee, most High, shall they be crowned.
Praised be my Lord for our Sister, the Bodily Death,
From the which no living man can flee.
Woe to them who die in mortal sin;
Blessed those who shall find themselves in Thy most holy will,
For the second death shall do them no ill.
Praise ye and bless ye my Lord, and give Him thanks,
And be subject to Him with great humility.*

In his last days and nights the troubadour of God asked to have
this song of the sun sung to him again and again. When Brother
Elias tried to make him understand that such a preparation for
death might be looked at askance by the people, Francis replied
smilingly: "Give me leave, Brother, to rejoice in the Lord and in
His praises and in my afflictions, for by the grace of the Holy Spirit
I am so conjoined and made one with the Lord that by His mercy
I may well be glad in Him, the Most High."[100]
Francis died as he had lived, with the melody of his divine sym-

---

* The text of the Canticle, here translated, is that of the Assisi MS. 338 (fol. 33),
and the translation itself is from P. Robinson, *The Writings of St. Francis of Assisi*,
152. As P. Robinson states, it is an attempt "to render literally into English the
naïf rhythm of the original Italian, which necessarily disappears in any formal
rhymed translation."

phony in his ears. *"Mortem cantando suscepit,"* says Celano, "singing he embraced death."[101]

It was Saturday, October 4, 1226. Evening twilight lay on the plains of Assisi. A large flock of larks, "which love the light and have a great fear of darkness," circled around the roof of the house for a long time with unusual liveliness and jubilant song. They were singing the evening song of him who had so often called on them to sing the praises of God.[102] *"Mortem cantando suscepit —* singing he embraced death." With the praises of his Lord sung by his feathered friends, the larks, echoing in his soul, he passed from the storm-tossed sea of this world to the eternal shores.

He had begun as an ardent pupil of the "joyous science"; he ended as a troubadour and minstrel of God. *"Mortem cantando suscepit —* singing he embraced death." In the life of this knight-errant of Christ there is nothing more chivalrous than his death.

Reference Notes

CHAPTER ONE

1. Cf. P. A. Weiss, O.P., *Die Entwicklung des christlichen Rittertums*, in: *Historisches Jahrbuch der Görresgesellschaft*, I (1880), pp. 107–140; Leon Gautier, *La Chevalerie* (Paris, 1884), p. 32 ff.; Roth von Schreckenstein, *Die Ritterwürde und der Ritterstand* (Freiburg i. Breisgau, 1886).

2. *Das Keyserrecht*, III, 4 ed. (Endemann, Cassel, 1846), p. 189.

3. Franz, *Die kirchlichen Benediktionen* (Freiburg i. Br., 1909), II, p. 293. Even today the "Benedictio novi militis" is found in the *Pontificale Romanum*.

4. *L'Ordene de Chevalerie*, ed. Barazan (Lausanne, 1759), p. 116.

5. Gautier, *loc. cit.*, p. 707.

6. "Chascun se soloit si et vanter et proisier: — Se ja Dex li donait Jursalem aprochier, — C'as dens mordroit les murs, s'il estoient d'achier." Gautier, *loc. cit.*, p. 71, n. 5.

7. "Encor me soit le poil elchié changié, — Si ferrai-je desor les renoiez. — Si je estoie en Paradis couchiez, — Si descendroie." Moniage Renoart, Gautier, *loc. cit.*, p. 71, n. 4.

8. Gautier, *loc. cit.*, p. 710.

9. Cf. Prutz, *Die geistlichen Ritterorden* (Berlin, 1908).

10. S. Bernardus Abbas, *De laude novae militiae*. Ad Milites Templi liber, c. 1, n. 1; Migne, *Patres latini*, t. 182, col. 921 f.

11. L. Gautier, *Les épopées francaises*, 2 ed. (Paris, 1892); P. Alexander Baumgartner, *Geschichte der Weltlitteratur*, V (Freiburg i. Br., 1905), pp. 15–39; E. Faral, *La chanson de Roland* (Paris, 1932); G. Bertoni, *La chanson de Roland* (Firenze, 1936); English translation into prose by I. Butler (Boston, 1904), and partly into verse by Way and Spenser (London, 1895).

12. *Das Rolandslied des Pfaffen Konrad*, ed. by Carl Wesle (Bonn, 1928).

13. G. Paris, *Les romans de table ronde*, in: *Histoire littéraire de la France*, XXX (Paris, 1888), pp. 1–270; Singer, *Die Artussage* (Bern und Leipzig, 1926); P. Anselm Salzer, *Illustrierte Geschichte der deutschen Litteratur*, I (Regensburg, 1926), pp. 139 ff.; Rhys, *Studies in the Arthurian Legend* (Oxford, 1891); Maynadier, *The Arthur of the English Poets* (Boston, 1907); Jones, *King Arthur in History and Legend* (Cambridge, 1911); Brown, *Ywain: A Study in the Origins of Arthurian Romance* (Boston, 1902).

14. Graudgent, C. H., *Outline of Phonology and Morphology of Old Provençal* (Boston, 1905); Paris, G., *Medieval French Literature* (London, 1902); Stimming, A., *Provenzalische Literatur*, in: Groeber, *Grundriss der romanischen Philologie*, II, 2 (Strassburg, 1897), pp. 1–69; A. Baumgartner, *loc. cit.*, V, pp. 125–151; Bertoni, G., *I trovatori d'Italia* (Modena, 1915); Anglade, *Les troubadours*, 2 ed.

(Paris, 1919); Bédier, J., *Les fabliaux* (Paris, 1925); R. Menéndez Pidal, *Poesia juglares y juglars* (Madrid, 1926); Jeanroy, A., *La poésie lyrique des troubadours* (Paris, 1934).

15. Cf. G. Ehrismann, *Geschichte der deutschen Litteratur*, 2. Teil, II, 1 (München, 1927), pp. 149, 279.

16. Baumgartner, *loc. cit.*, p. 37 ff.

17. Bédier, *Les légendes épiques*, II, pp. 139–278: *Les chansons de geste et les routes d'Italie.*

18. P. Rajna, *L'onomastica Italiana e l'epopea carolingia*, in: Romania, XVIII (1889), p. 65 ff.; G. Bertoni, *Il Duecento* (Milano, 1911), pp. 37–46; A. D'Ancona, *Le tradizioni Carolingie in Italia* (Livorno, 1913).

19. P. Rajna, *Un' iscrizione nepesina del 1131*, in: Arch. stor. ital., XVIII (1886), p. 329; S. *Francesco d'Assisi e gli spiriti cavalereschi*, in: Nuova Antologia, 249 (1926), p. 388.

20. P. Rajna, *Gli eroi brettoni nell' onomastica italiana del secolo XII*, in: Romania, XVII (1888), pp. 161, 355.

21. S. Colfi, *Atti e Memorie della Reale Deput. di Storia Patria per le prov. Mod.*, Serie III, Vol. IX, p. 133; Bertoni, *Atlante storico-paleografico del Duomo di Modena* (1909), tav. X.

22. Cf. Bertoni, *Il Duecento, loc. cit.*; A. Gaspary, *Storia della letteratura italiana tradotta dal tedesco da Nicola Zingarelli*, I (Torino, 1914), p. 107 f.

CHAPTER TWO

1. Gautier, *La Chevalerie*, p. 20 f.

2. Fortini, *Nova vita di San Francesco d'Assisi* (Milano, 1926), p. 43.

3. Celano, II, 3. Thomas of Celano, *Legenda prima et secunda*, and his *Tractatus de miraculis S. Francisci Assisiensis* are quoted according to the edition of the *Analecta Franciscana*, tav. X, the text and numbering of which agree with the edition of P. Edouard d'Alençon, O.M.C. (Rome: Desclée, Lefèbre et Soc., 1906). Quotations are made thus: Cel. I = *Legenda Prima;* Cel. II = *Legenda Secunda.* The arabic number refers to the running number of the editions.

4. Cel. I, 2; also Fortini, 42 f.

5. Cf. Fortini, 56 f., 162.

6. S. Bernardus Abbas, *De laude novae militiae,* c. 2, Opera ed. Migne, *Patres latini,* t. 182, col. 923.

7. F. Bourguelot, *Études sur les foires de Champagne aux XII, XIII et XIV siècles* (Paris, 1865); Bonfante, *Storia del commercio dei popoli latini del mediterraneo* (Torino, 1915), p. 293 ff.

8. Cel., II, 3.

9. Fortini, *loc. cit.*, p. 56, n. 19; Pio Rajna, *S. Francesco d'Assisi e gli spiriti cavallereschi*, in: *Nuova Antologia*, vol. 249 (Ottobre, 1926), p. 387; P. Michael Bihl, O.F.M., *De nomine S. Francisci*, in: *Archiv. franc. histor.*, XIX (1926), pp. 469–529.

10. Bonav. c. 15, n. 5. The *Legenda (maior) S. Francisci* of St. Bonaventure is quoted from the edition of Quaracchi (1898), with chapter and running number.

11. Cf. Faloci–Pulignani, *Dove andò a scuola S. Francesco?* In the periodical: *S. Francesco* (1925), p. 111 ff. Today the church of Santa Chiara rises where once stood the church of St. George. See also F. Pennacchi, *L'anno della prigionia di S. Francesco* (Perugia, 1915), p. 4.

12. Cf. Felder, *Geschichte der wissenschaftlichen Studien im Franziskanerorden* (Freiburg i. Br., 1904), p. 340.

13. Cf. Ozanam, *Documents inédits pour servir à l'histoire littéraire d'Italie du huitième au treizième siècle* (Paris, 1851), V, pp. 65–73.

14. Cel., I, 23; Bonav., XV, 5.

15. Cel., *Tract. de mirac.*, II, 3.

16. Cel., I, 22.

17. Cel., I, 100; II, 163; Eccleston, *De adventu Fratrum Minorum in Angliam,* coll. VI (ed. Little, Paris, 1909), p. 40. Eccleston says, however, that the Latin of Francis was faulty. (*. . . in qua fuit falsum latinum.*)

18. See for instance the "Office of the Passion of the Lord," which he composed of texts of the Vulgate and some additions of his own, *Opusc.,* pp. 126–148. The *Opuscula S. P. Francisci Assis.* are quoted from the edition of P. Leonard Lemmens, O.F.M. (Quaracchi, 1904), unless otherwise noted. This edition agrees, with the exception of a few minor details, with the edition of H. Boehmer: *Analekten zur Geschlichte des Franziskus von Assisi* (Tübingen, 1904), which is quoted whenever there is a discrepancy.

19. Cel., I, 16 II, 127; Soc., 10. The *Legenda Trium Sociorum* is quoted according to the edition of Faloci-Pulignani in *Miscellanea Francescana,* vol. VII, p. 81 ff., and in a special printing (Foligno, 1898).

20. Görres, *Der hl. Franziskus von Assisi ein Troubadour,* in: *Katholik,* XX (1826), p. 24 f.

21. Cel., I, 2; Socii, 2.

22. Cel., I, 2.

23. Gautier, *loc. cit.,* pp. 29, 131–134.

24. Socii, 3.

25. *Ibid.*

26. Bonav., I, 1.

27. Fortini, 115, n. 1, *Stat. del Comune di Assisi,* lib. 3, rub. 48.

28. Cel., I, 1–3; Soc., 1–2.

29. Cel., I, 2; II, 7; Soc., 7.

30. Soc., 2. 7.

31. Cel., II, 3; Socii, 3; P. Fredegando da Anversa (*L'allegra giovinezza di S. Francesco d'Assisi,* in: *L'Italia francescana,* I [1926], p. 273 ff.) proves conclusively that the youth of Francis was indeed a gay one, but in every respect morally pure.

32. Socii, 3; Bonav., I, 1.

33. Socii, 3.

34. Socii, 2.

35. Cel., II, 3.

36. Socii, 2.

37. See the analysis of the *geste* of Herviz of Metz in Gautier, *loc. cit.,* p. 213 ff., and also the sketch of the related *geste* of the Enfances Vivien.

38. Spec. perf., c. 4, 72. The *Speculum perfectionis status Fratris Minoris scil. Beati Francisci,* ed. Sabatier (Paris, 1898), is quoted: *Spec. Perf.,* with the running chapter numbers. English translation. *The Mirror of Perfection,* by Countess De La Warr (London: Burns and Oates, 1902).

CHAPTER THREE

1. The following local data are furnished by Fortini, *loc. cit.,* 21–57.

2. Wadding, *Annales,* vol. I, Apparatus, c. 4, n. 28.

3. This date has been definitively fixed by Fortini, 80 f., n. 10, although Fran-

cesco Pennacchi (*L'anno della prigionia di S. Francesco*, Perugia, 1915) still held
to the year 1204, as late as 1915.

4. Bonifazio da Verona, *L'Eulistea*, in Fortini, 73–75, 422.

5. Cel., II, 4; Socii, 4.

6. Ferrari, *Storia della rivoluzioni d'Italia*, I, 547.

7. Cel., II, 4.

8. Socii, 4.

9. Cel., II, 37.

10. Cel., II, 4; Socii, 4.

11. Cel., II, 4; Socii, 4.

CHAPTER FOUR

1. Cf. Fortini, 96.

2. Innocent III spent two weeks in Perugia in October, 1198. He died at Perugia
in 1216 and was entombed there. Bonazzi *Storia di Perugia*, I, 254.

3. Cf. the Papal letters to the consuls and the people of Assisi *"Mirari
cogimur,"* April 16, 1198, and *"Magnificavit Dominus,"* December, 1199, in
Potthast: *Regesta Pontificum Romanorum* I, p. 10, n. 10, and p. 88, n. 927. Also
Muratori: *Rerum Italicarum Scriptores* III, 1, p. 488.

4. See the letter of Innocent III to Bishop Guido of Assisi *"Sicut nobis tuis,"*
Potthast, I, p. 77, n. 821.

5. Odoricus Reynaldus: *Annales ecclesiastici ab anno quo desinit Caes. Baronius
continuati*, t. XIII, 122 (ad annum 1204), 77. On June 6, Pope Innocent III warned
the rulers and the people of Assisi in his letter *Gratum gerimus* (Potthast I, p. 193,
n. 2237): "that at no future time should they take an excommunicated person
or an enemy of the Church for an administrator of the city" (*ne postero tempore
excommunicatum vel ecclesiae inimicum ad civitatis regimen assumant*). Since
Girardo di Giliberto was consul from December, 1202, on, the interdict was undoubtedly imposed in the beginning of 1203. It was removed June 6, 1203.

6. Fortini, 87–98, 443.

7. Cf. *Gesta Innocentii III*, cap. XXX *sq.*, ed. Migne, t. 214, col. 54 *sqq.*;
Muratori, *Annali d'Italia* of the years 1200 to 1205; A. Luchaire, *Innocent III,
Rome et l'Italie* (Paris, 1904), p. 183 ff.

8. Regarding him see Huillard–Bréholles, *Historia diplomatica Friderici
Secundi*, I, 1, p. 48; *Gesta Innocentii III*, cap. XXVI, XXXII, XXXIV, col. 51,
56, 61. — That the royal chancellor as well as his brother, Count Gentile of
Manupello, were not inaccessible to intrigues and deceit, is only too evident from
the statements in the *Gesta Innocentii III*.

9. Cel., I, 4; Socii, 5.

10. Socii, 5.

11. Cel., II, 5; Socii, 6.

12. Cel., I, 5; II, 6; Socii, 5; Bonav., I, 3.

13. Socii, 5.

14. Socii, 6.

15. Cel., II, 6; Socii, 6.

CHAPTER FIVE

1. Socii, 6.

2. Cel., II, 7; Socii, 7.

3. Cel., I, 7; Socii, 12.

4. Cel., II, 8; Socii, 8–10.

5. Cel., II, 9; Socii, 11; Bonav., 15.
6. Cel., I, 17; II, 9; Socii, 11.
7. Cel., II, 9; Socii, 11; Bonav., 1, 5.
8. *Ibid.*
9. Cel., II, 10 f.; Socii, 13 f.; Bonav., 2, 1.
10. Louis Gillet, *Sur les pas de St. François d'Assise*, in: *Revue des Deux Mondes*, 96. année, 15 aout (1926), p. 756 f.
11. Emil Michael, *Kulturzustände des deutschen Volkes während des 13. Jahrhunderts* (Freiburg i. Br., 1903), pp. 238–240.
12. *Rolandslied* of Pfaffe Konrad V., 5159 f., 5169, 5820 ff.

CHAPTER SIX

1. Cel., I, 13; Socii, 18.
2. Cel., I, 11.
3. Socii, 12.
4. Fortini, 162, n. 5.
5. Socii, 19.
6. Cf. Fortini, 163, n. 10.
7. Cel., I, 13–15; Socii, 19–20; Bonav., 2, 4.
8. At any rate between February 22 and March 19. Cf. P. Dominic Mandic, *De legislatione antiqua O.FF. Minorum* I (Mostar, 1923), 4–19.
9. *Divine Comedy*, "Paradise," Canto XI, transl. by H. F. Cary (New York: Cassel Publishing Co.).

CHAPTER SEVEN

1. Bonav., 2, 4.
2. Bonav., 2, 5.
3. Cel., I, 15.
4. Cel., I, 16. According to tradition this really happened in the neighborhood of Caprignone. Cf. P. Nicola Cavanna, *L'Umbria francescana illustrata* (Perugia, 1910), p. 190 ff.; Lucarelli, *Memoria a guida di Gubbio* (1888), p. 583.
5. Cel., I, 17; Bonav., 2, 6.
6. Opusc., 77.
7. Cel., I, 21; Jord., n. 1.
8. Cel., II, 14; Socii, 21–24.
9. Anonym. Perusin., ed. *Miscell. francesc.* IX, 37, n. 9.
10. Socii, 23.
11. Regarding this name of the brother of Francis see Cristofani, *Storie di Assisi*, I, p. 78 ff.; *Acta Sanctorum*, Oct., tom. II, 556; *Archiv. francisc.* I, 248 ff.
12. Cel., II, 12; Socii, 23.
13. Cel., II, 13; Socii, 24.
14. Regarding the probable amount of work done by Francis on St. Damian's see P. Leone Bracalone, O.F.M., *Storia di San Damiano* (Assisi, 1919), p. 60.
15. Bonav., 2, 7.
16. The historicity of these accounts cannot, of course, be proved. Cf. Edouard d' Alençon, *Des origines de l'Eglise de la Portiuncule*, in: *Études Franc.* XI (1904), 585–606; Fr. Octavius a San Francisco: *Archivium Portiunculae*, ed. Aegidius M. Guisto, S. Mariae Angelorum (1916), 10.
17. Cel., I, 21; Bonav., 2, 8.
18. Cel., II, 11.
19. Wadding, *Annal. ad a. 1213*, n. 17.

20. Proofs in Lud. Lipsin, *Compendiosa historia vitae S. P. Francisci* (Assisi, 1756), 19, and also in Faloci–Pulignani: *Miscellanea franc.*, vol. II, 33–37.

21. Spec. perf., c. 56.

22. *Test., Opusc.*, 78 *sq.*

CHAPTER EIGHT

1. Cf. Ducange–Carpenterius, *Glossarium ad Scriptores mediae et infimae latinitatis*, under *Praeco, Praeconare, Praeconari.*

2. Heliand. According to the Old Saxon by Paul Herrmann (Leipzig), Reclam jun., verse 1296 f.

3. Heliand, verses 4737, 4870, 4872, 3102, 4602, 3393–3399.

4. Cel., I, 22; Socii, 25; Bonav., 3, 1.

5. Jord. a Jano, *Chronica*, ed. Boehmer (Paris, 1908), n. 2.

6. Cel., I, 23.

7. *Ibid.*

8. Socii, 28 ss.; Cel., I, 24; II, 15; Bonav., 3, 3–4.

9. Socii, 33.

10. Cel., I, 25, 29; Socii, 35.

11. Socii, 36.

12. Socii, 37–45.

13. Socii, 46.

14. Anon. Perusin., *Legenda S. Francisci*, ed. P. van Ortroy, in: *Miscell. franc.*, IX, n. 33; cf. Socii, 48.

15. Cel., II, 17; Socii, 51.

16. Socii, 51.

17. Socii, 52.

18. Socii, 33, 37. Likewise Brother Leo in the *Vita fr. Aegidii*, ed. Analecta franc., III, 76.

19. Socii, 54.

20. Socii, *ibid.*

21. Cel., I, 36–37.

22. Socii, 57.

23. *Jacobi Vitriacensis Epistula data Jan. a. 1216 Oct.*, ed. Boehmer, *Analekten*, 98 *sq.*

24. For further details see Felder, *Ideals of St. Francis of Assisi* (Benziger Bros.), p. 309 f.

25. Cel., I, 89, 120.

26. Regarding the missionary journeys of Francis see P. Odulphus van der Vat, *Die Anfänge der Franziskanermissionen und ihre Weiterentwicklung im nahen Orient* (Werl i. Westf., 1934), 39–59.

27. Cel., I, 55; *Tract. de Mirac.*, 33.

28. Cel., I, 55; Bonav., 9, 5.

29. Cel., I, 56.

30. For the sources on this mission journey and its progress and outcome *cf.* Girolamo Golubovich, *Bibliotheca bio-bibliographica della Terra Santa e dell' Oriente Francescano*, I (Quaracchi, 1906), 1 ff.; Lemmens, *De Sancto Francisco praedicante coram Sultano Aegypti*, in: *Arch. franc. histor.*, XIX (1926), 559–578; P. Odulphus van der Vat, *loc cit.*, 51–59.

31. Jord., 10.

32. Bonav., 9, 7.

33. Wadding, *Annal. Minor. ad a. 1220*, 38. Regarding this martyrdom *cf.*

Odulphus van der Vat, *loc cit.*, 46–49.

34. *Opusc.*, 43–48.

35. *Opusc.*, 71, 73 *sq.*

36. Cel., II, 152.

37. Gautier, *La Chevalerie*, 71.

38. *"Tous les mauvais resteront par deçà, ceux qui n'aiment ni Dieu, ni bien, ni honneur, ni valeur: . . . les morveux, les couards resteront."* Jos. Bédier, *Les chansons de croisade* (Paris, 1909), 173.

39. *"Chevalier en ce monde–ici — Ne peuvent vivre sans souci. — Ils doivent le peuple défendre — et leur sang pour la foi espandre."* Gautier, *La Chevalerie*, 46.

40. *Rolandslied des Pfaffen Konrad*, verses 227–232. The primitive text was edited by Carl Wesle (Bonn, 1928). Also: *La chanson de Roland*, verses 1129–1134, 1518–1523, ed. Jos. Bédier (Paris, 1922), pp. 88, 117. The above version in English is by the translator.

41. *La Chanson de Roland*, ed. Jos. Bédier, verses 3666–3674.

CHAPTER NINE

1. Cel., I, 7; Socii, 11; Bonav., 1, 5.

2. Cel., I, 55.

3. Bonav., 1, 5; 2, 2; 9, 7; 13, 9–10.

4. Wadding, *Annales ad a. 1210*. Cf. the *Actus beati Francisci in valle Reatina*, ed. Franc. Pennacchi, in: *Miscellanea franc.*, XIII (1911), 8.

5. *Vita Fr. Aegidii*, ed. *Anal. francisc.*, III (1897), 75.

6. *Loc. cit.*, 78

7. *Spec. perf.*, 72.

8. Wolfram von Eschenbach, *Parzifal*, IX, 888–890. Cf. *Tristan*, V, 5027 f., 5048; *Song of Roland*, 1975–1977. English version by the translator.

9. *Chanson de Roland*, 1820 ff., 3338 ff., 3831 f., 3964 ff.; *Rolandslied*, 6114 ff., 9009 ff.

10. *Rolandslied*, 2378 ff., 2398 ff.

11. Deut. 12: 17.

12. "I have given you an example, that as I have done, so you also should do" (John 13:15).

13. "He who does not . . . follow Me, is not worthy of Me" (Matt., 10:38).

14. *Regulae antiquissimae*, in: Boehmer, *Analekten zur Geschichte des hl. Franziskus von Assisi* (Tübingen, 1904), 88; Vlastimil Kybal, *Die Ordensregeln des hl. Franz von Assisi* (Leipzig, 1915), 11; Paschal Robinson, *The Writings of St. Francis of Assisi* (Philadelphia, 1906), p. 25 ff.

15. Reg. I, c. 22, 23; *Opusc.*, 56, 60; Robinson, *The Writings*, p. 55 ff.

16. *Ultima voluntas quam scripsit sororibus S. Clarae*, Boehmer, 35; Robinson, 75 ff.

17. Cel., I, 84; II, 26.

18. Joseph Goerres, *Der heilige Franziskus von Assisi, ein Troubadour* (Strassburg, 1826), 53.

19. Socii, 68.

20. *Epist. ad Capit. gener.*, *Opusc.*, ed. Boehmer, 57; Robinson, *Writings*, p. 109 ff.

21. Cel., I, 115.

22. Boehmer, 71, places this prayer *Absorbeat*, which was attested for the first time by Ubertino of Casale (1305) among the "dubia." Cf. Robinson, *Writings*, p. 145.

23. Cel., I, 71.

24. Cel., I, 84.

25. Emil Michael, *Kulturzustände des deutschen Volkes während des 13. Jahrhunderts* (Freiburg i. Br., 1903), pp. 238–240.

26. *Les chansons de croisade publiées par Joseph Bédier* (Paris, 1909), 33, IV. and V. strophe.

27. *Loc. cit.*, 193, IV. strophe.

28. *Loc. cit.*, 21, III. strophe; 290, III. strophe. These and similar Old-French songs can be given in English only in prose.

29. Bernardus Abbas, *De laude novae militiae. Ad milites Templi liber*, ed. Migne, *PP. lat.*, 192, col. 921–940.

30. "*Crucifixi milites. . . . Haec enim militia caeli et terrae typo praefigurata sola et praecipua esse videtur, quae vicem Christi in opprobrio suae crucis doleat et terram sanctam Christianis debitam recuperare ab oppressione gentilium se devovit.*" Perlbach, *Die Statuten des deutschen Ordens* (Halle a. s. [1890], 23 f.).

31. Bonav., I, 5.

32. Cel., II, 10 f.

33. Socii, 14; Spec. perf., c. 92. Cf. Cel., II, 11.

34. Cel., *Tract. de mirac.*, 2.

35. Cel., *ibid.*, 2; Bonav., *Leg. de mir.*, 1, 2.

36. Cel., *ibid.*

37. *Actus b. Francisci et Sociorum eius*, ed. Sabatier (Paris, 1902), c. 38, n. 5.

38. Socii, 37.

39. *Opusc.*, 77; Robinson, *Writings*, p. 81 f.

40. *Opusc.*, 126–148; Robinson, *Writings*, pp. 154–176.

41. *Opusc.*, 126; Robinson, *Writings*, p. 155.

42. *Opusc.*, 148; Robinson, *Writings*, p. 176.

43. Cel., I, 103.

44. *Ibid.*

45. Cel., I, 97.

46. Cel., I, 98, 99, 103, 105, 108; II, 44, 64, 126, 166; *Tract de mir.*, 14.

47. Cel., I, 105, 107.

48. Bonav., 14, 2.

49. "*In cruce perseverans ad sublimium spirituum gradum meruit advolare. Semper enim in cruce fuit. . . .*" Cel., I, 115.

50. *Epistula fratris Eliae de transitu s. Francisci, loc. cit.*, of the *AA.SS.* and Lempe, Boehmer.

CHAPTER TEN

1. Dante: *Paradise*, Canto XI.

2. Cel., II, 55.

3. Socii, 27–29; Cel., I, 24.

4. *Opusc.*, 79.

5. Socii, 33, 40.

6. Socii, 46; Cel., I, 32.

7. Cel., I, 32.

8. Cel., I, 32–34; Socii, 46–53.

9. Socii, 50.

10. Socii, 51.

11. Cel., I, 34.

12. Socii, 35.

13. Bonav., c. 7, n. 2.
14. Cel., II, 70.
15. Bonav., c. 7, n. 5.
16. Cel., II, 70.
17. *Opusc.*, 20.
18. Bonav., c. 7, n. 6; Cel., II, 82.
19. Cel., II, 55.
20. Cel., II, 216; Spec. perf., c. 87.
21. Dante: *Paradise*, Canto XI.
22. *Test., Opusc.*, 79.
23. Socii, 29.
24. Cel., II, 216.
25. Socii, 51.
26. Socii, 48.
27. Iacobi Vitriac., *Historia orientalis*, lib. 2, c. 32, in Boehmer: *Analekten*, 102.
28. Spec. perf., c. 107.
29. Cel., II, 55.
30. *Opusc.*, 75.
31. *Opusc.*, 18, 20 f.
32. Bonav., 7, 1. Cf. Cel., II, 200.
33. Francesco Tresatti: *Le poesie spirituali del B. Jacopone da Todi* (Venetia, 1617), 351–353.
34. Cel., II, 82.
35. Cel., II, 93.
36. *Salutatio virtutum, Opusc.*, 21.
37. *Actus*, c. 13, n. 22 f.
38. Cel., II, 216.
39. Dante: *Paradise*, Canto XI.
40. Cel., II, 55.
41. *Opusc.*, 76.
42. Socii, 8.
43. Cel., II, 83.
44. Bonav., 7, 1.
45. Cel., II, 199; Socii, 15; Bonav., 7, 1.
46. Bonav., 7, 7.
47. Socii, 28.
48. *Regula*, I, c. 9; *Opusc.*, 36 f.
49. *Regula*, II, c. 6; *Opusc.*, 68 f.

CHAPTER ELEVEN

1. *The Knighthood of the Middle Ages According to Its Political and Military Constitution*, De la Curne de Sainte-Palaye.
2. "*Car d'armes est li mestier tiex: Bruit es chant et joie à l'ostel*," loc. cit.
3. Cel., I, 7.
4. Socii, 11.
5. Socii, 13.
6. Cel., I, 93.
7. Spec. perf., c. 95.
8. Cel., I, 23.
9. Bonav., *Leg. minor*, ed. Quaracchi (1898), 236.
10. Socii, 22.

11. Spec. perf., c. 121.

12. Cel., I, 2; Socii, 2.

13. Cel., I, 93.

14. Cel., II, 126.

15. Cel., *Vita S. Clarae*, c. 6, n. 51, Act. SS., Augusti, t. II, 764.

16. "Vita Fr. Aegidii," *Anal. franc.*, III, 103 f.

17. Cel., II, 82, 106, 273; Spec. perf., c. 100; cf. U. Cosmo, *Frate Pacifico, "rex versuum,"* in: *Gior. Stor. di letteratura ital.*, XXXVIII (1901), 1–40.

18. Spec. perf., c. 121; *Actus*, c. 18.

19. Several scholars have already pointed to this urge for acting in Francis: H. Boehmer, *Analekten*, XLIX–LI; Fr. Remigius Boving, O.F.M., *Arch. Franc. hist.*, XIX (1926), 617 ff.; Louis Gillet, *"Sur les pas de S. Francois d'Assise,"* in: *Revue des Deux Mondes*, t. XXXV, 322 ff.; Hilarin Felder, *The Ideals of St. Francis of Assisi*, 343–347; Fr. Cuthbert, O.F.M.Cap., *The Romanticism of St. Francis* (London: Longmans, Green and Co., 1915), pp. 19, 20, 66.

20. Cel., II, 8.

21. Cel., I, 52.

22. Cel., II, 61.

23. Cel., I, 84–86.

24. Cel., I, 83; II, 107.

25. Thomas Spalatensis archidiaconus, *Historia Salonitarum*, ed. *Monum. Germ. hist.*, XXIX, 580. Thomas met Francis in 1222.

26. Bonav., c. 12, n. 8.

27. Cel., I, 97.

28. Cel., II, 73.

29. Cel., II, 127.

30. *Loc. cit.*

31. *Analekten*, XLIX, LI. Similarly Faloci–Pulignani, *Conferenze francescane*, Città di Castello (1924), 263.

32. "Der hl. Franziskus von Assisi, ein Troubadour," in: *Katholik*, XX (1826), 25.

33. *Lehrbuch der Dogmengeschichte*, III, 382.

34. *Geschichte der Weltliteratur*, VI: *Die italienische Literatur*, 62 f., 64, 68.

35. We have adduced elaborate proofs of this in our work: *Geschichte der wissenschaftlichen Studien im Franziskanerorden*, 426–447. Cf. Fr. Antoine de Serent, O.F.M., "L'Ame franciscaine," in: *Arch. franc. hist.*, VIII (1913), 454–458. See also *Catholic Encycl.* under "Hymns" and "Hymnody."

36. Baumgartner, *loc. cit.*

37. *De vulgari eloquentia*, lib. I, c. 10, ed. Pio Rajna, in: *Le Opere di Dante*, Testo critico della Società dantesca italiana, 329.

38. See above.

39. Actus b. Franc., c. 9, n. 8.

40. Actus, *loc. cit.*

41. Socii, 10.

42. Cel., II, 13.

43. Cel., I, 16.

44. Socii, 33; *Vita fratris Aegidii*, ed. *Anal. Franc.*, III, 76.

45. Cel., II, 127.

46. S. Bernardinus, *Opera*, t. IV (Venetiis, 1561), Sermo IV, XVI. Cf. A. Tenneroni, *Inizi di antiche poesie italiane* (Firenze, 1909), 124.

47. P. Ireneo Affò: *Dei Cantici Volgari di San Francesco di Assisi* (Guastalla, 1777).

48. Goerres, "Der hl. Franz von Assisi als Troubadour," in: *Katholik*, XX (1826), 1–13; A. F. Ozanam, *Les poets franciscains en Italie au treizième siècle* (Paris, 1852); Fr. Schlosser, *Die Lieder des hl. Franziskus von Assisi* (Frankfurt a.M., 1842); Gian Franc. Gamurrini, *Alcuni versi volgari di S. Francesco d'Assisi* (Cortona e Roma, 1901); Paschal Robinson, *The Writings of St. Francis of Assisi*, (The Dolphin Press, 1906), 183 f.

49. A reliable treatment of this question is given by Faloci–Pulignani, *Conferenze Francescane*, 254–260.

50. *Opusc.*, 20.

51. *Opusc.*, 119–123.

52. *Opusc.*, 87–115.

53. *Opusc.*, 126–148.

54. *Opusc.*, 50 f. Regarding the above quoted writings see P. Robinson, O.F.M., *The Writings of St. Francis of Assisi.*

55. Monaci, *Crestomazia italiana dei primi secoli* (Città di Castello, 1912), characterizes the *Canticle of the Sun* as "rhymed or assonant prose."

56. Cel., I, 16.

57. Socii, 21.

58. Cel., I, 24.

59. Socii, 30.

60. Socii, 33.

61. See Felder–Bittle, *The Ideals of St. Francis of Assisi*, 388 ff., 403 f.

62. *Opusc.*, 119–123.

63. Socii, 15.

64. Socii, 46.

65. Socii, 58.

66. Eccleston, *De adventu Fratrum Minorum in Angliam*, coll. VI, ed. Little (Paris, 1909), 40.

67. *Reg.*, I, c. 21, 23; *Opusc.*, 50. 61.

68. *Epist.* quam misit ad omnes custodes, *Opusc.*, 114.

69. G. Schnuerer, *Franz von Assisi* (Munich, 1907), 113.

70. Spec. perf., c. 100.

71. Cel., II, 217.

72. In the non-Franciscan literature of *Lauds*, too, the praise of Mary assumes an important place. Proof of this lies in the *laud* texts published by A. Bartoli (*Crestomazia della Poesia italiana del periodo delle origini*, Torino, 1882) and by Monaci (*Crestomazia, loc. cit.*, 456, 461, 471, etc.).

73. Cel., I, 21; Bonav., c. 2, n. 8. Cf. P. Athanasius Bierbaum, O.F.M., *Der hl. Franziskus und die Gottesmutter* (Paderborn, 1904).

74. *Epist.* ad Capit. Gen., *Opusc.*, 102; *Bonav.*, c. 9, n. 3.

75. Cel., II, 198.

76. *Opusc.*, 105, 121.

77. *Opusc.*, 119, 126.

78. Cel., II, 198.

79. Cel., I, 24.

80. *Opusc.*, 128.

81. "Salutatio beatae Mariae Virginis," *Opusc.*, 123. Cf. P. Robinson, *The Writings*, 143 f.

82. F. Pellegrini, *La Canzone d'amore di Guido Guinizelli,* in: *Studi Medievali,* I (1923), 9 ff.

83. E. Barrana, *La Gerusalemme celeste e la Babilonia infernale di Giacomino da Verona* (Verona, 1921); E. J. May, *De Jerusalem celesti* and *De Babilonia infernali* (Firenze, 1930).

84. Hilarin Felder, *Jacopones Marienminne* (Stanz, 1903).

85. Cf. C. Underhill, *Jacopone da Todi* (London, 1919), a biography of the poet, with English translation of selected poems by Mrs. T. Beck.

86. G. Bertoni, *loc. cit.,* 128.

87. Cel., I, 80; II, 165.

88. Cel., I, 81.

89. Cel., II, 168.

90. Cel., II, 171.

91. Cel., I, 59

92. Cel., I, 58.

93. Cel., I, 115.

94. *Litterae* quas misit omnibus fidelibus, *Opusc.,* 94 f.

95. Cel., II, 213; Spec. perf., c. 100.

96. Spec. perf., c. 119.

97. Spec. perf., c. 100.

98. Spec. perf., c. 101.

99. Spec. perf., c. 123.

100. Cel., I, 109; Spec. perf., c. 121.

101. Cel., II, 214.

102. Bonav., 14, 6.